Slouching Towards Los Angeles

Slouching Towards Los Angeles

Living and Writing by Joan Didion's Light

EDITED BY STEFFIE NELSON

Rare Bird Books
Los Angeles, Calif.

Rare Bird
453 South Spring Street, Suite 302
Los Angeles, CA 90013
rarebirdbooks.com

For more information, address:
Rare Bird Books Subsidiary Rights Department
453 South Spring Street, Suite 302
Los Angeles, CA 90013

Set in Minion
Printed in the United States

10 9 8 7 6 5 4 3 2 1

Publisher's Cataloging-in-Publication Data

Names: Nelson, Steffie, editor.
Title: Slouching Towards Los Angeles: Living and Writing
by Joan Didion's Light / edited by Steffie Nelson.
Description: Includes bibliographical references. | First Hardcover Edition. |
A Genuine Rare Bird Book | New York, NY; Los Angeles, CA:
Rare Bird Books, 2020.
Identifiers: ISBN 9781644280676
Subjects: LCSH Didion, Joan—Criticism and Interpretation. | California—
In Literature. | American Prose Literature—20th Century—History and
Criticism. | BISAC LITERARY CRITICISM / American / General.
Classification: LCC PS3554.I33 N46 2020 | DDC 813/.54—dc23

Contents

Introduction

IN *THE WHITE ALBUM*, Joan Didion famously wrote that "a place belongs forever to whoever claims it hardest, remembers it most obsessively...loves it so radically that he remakes it in his image"[1]—criteria that made California hers for all time. *Slouching Towards Los Angeles* is a celebration and an investigation of Didion's ongoing claim on California and its writers—because she, in turn, belongs to us.

This collection began as a literary event I organized in summer 2015 with the arts organization LAND (Los Angeles Nomadic Division), as part of their Manifest Destiny Billboard Project. A collaboration with the artist Zoe Crosher, this project examined the history of territorial expansion and the promise of the West via billboard art interventions in ten cities, spanning the I-10 freeway from coast to coast. Santa Monica was the final stop, and the idea was to explore similar themes, taking native daughter Joan Didion—whose California writing encompasses everything from the Donner Party to The Doors—as a touchstone.

Based on my own experience of Didion—both her writing and her example—as linked to the visceral pull of Los Angeles

(I relocated from New York in 2005), and the conversations I'd had with other writers who also migrated to the City of Angels with their creased copies of *Slouching Towards Bethlehem*, I began to think that every writer in Los Angeles probably had something to say about Joan Didion. Maybe there was an essay or concept that felt especially resonant; a shared obsession; or it could simply be an image of the author that left an indelible impression and sparked the imagination.

I started reaching out to writers I knew and admired, inviting them to take a look at Didion's legacy and influence through the lens of personal experience and against the larger backdrop of the West. With very few exceptions, everyone enthusiastically agreed to participate; several people told me they had been waiting years to write these particular pieces. The fifteen LA writers and artists who read their essays for a rapt crowd in a divinely Didionesque Brentwood backyard has expanded to twenty-five in this collection—including two East Coast inhabitants and one Mexico City dweller.

Like Didion, most of the contributors (myself included) are or have been, at one time or another, working journalists— writing to deadlines and word counts, striving to discover that subject and angle which make a story greater than the sum of its parts, all while still filing by Monday morning. Some of us have moved on to novels or nonfiction books, screenplays or podcasts, some of us continue to write for newspapers, magazines, and websites, some of us teach. What we share is an understanding of a vocation that is often rigid and unforgiving—and a sense of awe and a deep respect for Didion's ability to consistently make it art. We marvel that her gender was at once revolutionary and irrelevant; she wasn't a woman playing a man's game—she created her own game. Twenty of this book's twenty-five contributors are women, a ratio she helped make possible.

♦♦♦

Joan Didion grew up in Sacramento, went to college in Berkeley, and then, after a stint in New York City during which she worked at *Vogue* and met her husband, John Gregory Dunne, she returned to California in 1964 to live for twenty-four years in Los Angeles. These years were ones of radical change—from the rise of the counterculture through the Reagan era—and in that time Didion became the city's most important public intellectual, elevating LA beyond Hollywood and Hollywood beyond itself. She held California up like a diamond, revealing each facet (and flaw) through meticulous and surprising detail, startling psychological insights, and prose so clean it's incandescent.

In a 1977 *Ms.* magazine interview, Didion described being compelled by subjects that started as pictures in her mind that possessed a certain shimmer around the edges. She compared this effect to the way schizophrenics or those under the influence of psychedelic drugs are said to see the world, when the molecular structure starts to break down. "Writing is the attempt to understand what's going on in the shimmer,"[2] she said.

I believe that the shimmer is a crystallization of some truth, her truth, and that Didion's writing transmits these truths to us. Through her words we enter the shimmer, the place where the molecular structure breaks down and perception is porous, and we emerge with both a new way of seeing and maybe a new way of writing.

Slouching Towards Los Angeles is love letter and thank you note, personal memoir and social commentary, cultural history and literary critique. It offers a portrait of a writer and her readers that is as multifaceted as the work that inspired it—and perhaps a little schizophrenic, too. Each author finds a unique entry point.

Some meet Didion on the LA freeways or Franklin Avenue. Others are more connected through inner landscapes. Some gaze at a photograph—a fleeting instant captured in Hollywood or Malibu—until it speaks its truth. A few enter through side doors like Didion's recipe collection and the Sacramento state archives. Still others share personal histories that take us to Brentwood's Mandeville Canyon and San Francisco's Haight-Ashbury, after the hippies.

Of course, Joan Didion said "goodbye to all that" California dreaming in 1988, returning to New York where she has lived ever since on the Upper East Side. But her last three books—*The Year of Magical Thinking, Blue Nights,* and *South and West*—all circled back to California, to that formative, fertile time for the writer and her family, now shadowed with tragedy.

I recently watched footage of an interview Didion did at the New York Public Library in late 2011, after the release of *Blue Nights.* At the very end, the interviewer, Sloane Crosley, asked what was bringing her joy, and Didion responded that it was the same things that had always brought her joy: the small things. Then she added, her dry delivery belying the delight darting behind her eyes, "Well, sometimes they're really big things, like the sun going down over the Pacific brought me joy last week."[3]

And just like that, she is here, staring at the same sun, at the edge of the same coast, pondering the same eternity and experiencing the same joy, as us.

Steffie Nelson
Los Angeles, August 2019

ENDNOTES:

1. Joan Didion, "In the Islands," in *The White Album* (New York: Simon & Schuster, 1979), 146.
2. Susan Braudy, "A Day in the Life of Joan Didion," *Ms.*, February 1977.
3. Joan Didion, interview with Sloane Crosley at the New York Public Library, November 21, 2011, video. https://www.nypl.org/audiovideo/joan-didion-conversation-sloane-crosley

Hello to All This

By Ann Friedman

On a Saturday night last year, I found myself in a karaoke bar at 3:45 a.m., participating in a raucous group rendition of "New York, New York." This represented a certain amount of personal growth. "Not really liking New York" has long been part of who I am, even though some of my best friends live there and it is ostensibly the center of my professional universe. My take has long been, "Why would I want to make it there when I could make it anywhere else?"

I spent the worst year of my life in New York—the *Reality Bites* phase right after graduation. I moved from Missouri to join my college boyfriend, who had landed *my* dream job at *The New York Times*. I found quasi-employment in the form of an internship at a nonprofit, where I wrote press releases and assembled annual reports, carefully selecting stock photos of the most "real" looking women and children to accompany bleak statistics about domestic violence.

I was not in New York because I had something to prove, nor because I wanted to draw some lines around a blurry fantasy of city life. I was there because I couldn't think of anywhere else to go. New York was someone else's story that I halfheartedly inhabited because I was painfully aware that I hadn't yet written my own. I didn't meet interesting people. I didn't do interesting drugs. I did not walk through Washington Square Park at dawn, or stumble into a cab, laughing, to get out of the driving rain. I did not take cabs. Ever. I was broke—not in a Patti Smith and Robert Mapplethorpe starving-artist kind of way. In a "staying home and watching DVDs and eating stir-fry" kind of way.

So I didn't say "Goodbye to All That." I just said goodbye.

In Joan Didion's parting note to the city she loved at twenty-three, originally published as "Farewell to the Enchanted City" in the *Saturday Evening Post*, she writes, "I do not mean 'love' in any colloquial way. I mean that I was in love with the city, the way you love the first person who ever touches you and you never love anyone quite that way again."[1]

New York and me? We were always meant to be platonic.

New York is the prom king. He knows he's great, and he's gonna make it really hard on you if you decide you want to love him. I opted out. And from my now-comfortable perch on the dry and cracking western edge of this continent, I look back at friends who have stuck things out with New York and think, "*How? Why?*"

For one thing, they share a willingness to consider New York from a cinematic distance, overlooking the city's many irritants except insofar as they add grit and drama to their personal story. In day-to-day terms, this manifests as complaining vigorously about subway hardships and bedbug plagues, and then posting Instagram photos of the skyline at sunset. A not insignificant number of the New York lovers I know—especially the twenty-somethings—are actually pretty unhappy day-to-day. I picture the prom king's date sitting near him at a party, ignored but still kind of proud to be in the room and on his arm—and incredibly offended at the suggestion that she should break up with him for someone who dotes on her more.

Oh, how California *dotes*! Sun yourself. Take the car. Let your guard down. Breathe deeply, and you'll smell the jasmine and dusty sage. Show up twenty minutes late. (Just text "Sorry—traffic.") Explore the weirder corners of your spirituality. Describe yourself, without sarcasm, as a writer *slash* creative entrepreneur. Work from home. Spread out. Wear the comfortable pants.

When I describe this sunshine-and-avocado-filled existence to some New Yorkers, they acknowledge that they really like California, too, but could never move here because they'd get too "soft." At first this confused me, but after hearing it a few times, I've come to believe that a lot of people equate comfort with complacency, calmness with laziness. If you're happy, you're not working hard enough. You've stopped striving.

Didion writes, "I talk about how difficult it would be for us to 'afford' to live in New York right now, about how much 'space' we need. All I mean is that I was very young in New York, and that at some point the golden rhythm was broken, and I am not that young anymore."[2]

I'm not young anymore, either. It's impossible for me to know if my California life is so much better than my brief New York tryst because I've simply grown up and worked my way into a better phase of my career, or whether coming to California was what allowed me to find happiness and success. These things are inextricable. What I do know is that I'm still striving. And I didn't lose a golden rhythm back East; I found it out West.

ENDNOTES:

1. Joan Didion, "Goodbye to All That," in *Slouching Towards Bethlehem* (New York: Farrar, Straus and Giroux, 1968), 228.
2. Didion, "Goodbye to All That," 238.

How to Find Your Place in Life, or What I Learned from Joan Didion's "On Keeping a Notebook"

By Jori Finkel

FLAUBERT ONCE SAID THAT a lady is not a lady more than one hundred feet from her carriage, and the way that he punished Madame Bovary for her dreams and affairs, stripping her of her money, health, and sanity alike, would seem to illustrate that point.

I read that line from Flaubert in college. But Joan Didion was the first writer I read who said something similar in terms that made sense for me personally as a teenage girl who felt—like so many teenagers everywhere—painfully displaced in her small, almost suburban, and dreadfully boring Midwestern town.

"You are just in the wrong place," Didion whispered to me in so many words.

She said it in "Goodbye to All That," describing the feeling of carrying a container of coffee from Chock Full o' Nuts or the rhythms of putting out a fashion magazine, remembering when

New York felt like the right place for her before she found out "it is distinctly possible to stay too long at the fair."[1]

And she said it in her essay "On Keeping a Notebook"—which has obvious appeal as a how-to primer for any aspiring writer who likes to eavesdrop but which also delivers an unexpected meditation on identity and place. I was in the right place until it was the wrong place, she says of herself. Or to me: There is nothing wrong with you; you are just in the wrong place.

This idea that there is a right place and time for each of us, and you can vacate it by mistake and return to it only at great expense, fills much of her work with a kind of anticipatory nostalgia—looking backward even as she projects into the future. It's an example of what Shakespeare called the "preposterous," which as his scholars love to point out literally describes a condition where "before" follows "after" or "pre" follows "post"—a state of chronological, and often psychological, confusion.

Remember the scene in "On Keeping a Notebook" when Didion sees a blonde in a Pucci bathing suit at the Beverly Hills Hotel surrounded by fat men? The blonde does the one thing that a blonde in a Pucci bathing suit was born to do: she "arches one foot and dips it into the pool."[2] There, she's in her element. Right time, right place. It has a cinematic or photographic quality, like Henri Cartier-Bresson's decisive moment.

Then in New York some years later, when Didion happens to spot the same woman coming out of Saks Fifth Avenue, the magic is gone. She looks tired and her mink coat is not *au courant*, not done in the style they were doing that year. "In the harsh wind that day she looked old and irrevocably tired to me,"[3] she writes.

Irrevocable is a favorite Didion word. Once you leave it or lose it, you can't get it back. In California, this blonde is beautiful. In New York, she's haggard.

Then there's the subject of Didion's first recorded story, which she tells us she wrote at age five in a notebook that her mother gave her in hopes she would stop whining and start to write it all down instead. The story features a woman who "believed herself to be freezing to death in the Arctic night, only to find, when day broke, that she had stumbled onto the Sahara Desert, where she would die of the heat before lunch."[4]

What is this woman's problem? For one, she doesn't know where she is.

Sure, you can read Didion's sensitivity to being displaced as a sign of her own neurotic or depressive tendencies—and she is the first to admit that a well-adjusted person would never need to keep a notebook in the first place.

You can also read her attention to displacement as a form of political alienation, reflecting a generational loss of innocence—often associated with the political upheavals of the 1960s—that gives so much of her writing its moodiness.

But when I was a teenager in the 1980s in Libertyville, Illinois, population 17,465 and not one of them interested me, I read it differently: as a command to find the right city for me, to find my people.

I didn't want to die of heat exhaustion in the cultural desert of my childhood. And I didn't want to be tired and haggard like the Pucci girl in New York. I wanted to be like the Pucci girl in Beverly Hills—perfectly at home in her element, only bikinis were not what I had in mind.

What I dreamed about was Manhattan, as Joan Didion wrote about it: the land of fashion magazines and jasmine soap from Henri Bendel and drinking until the sun rises and there is no ice left for the drinks.

By the time I was a senior at Libertyville High School in Libertyville, Illinois, my family was in free fall financially and just two years away from losing our home to foreclosure. But probably fueled by a growing sense of helplessness, my mom had the idea that we should have one last vacation during my spring break, and she found a cheap hotel in Laguna Beach for a week. For my brother, who was a thirteen-year-old skate punk just learning to surf, Orange County was heaven. For me, it was closer to hell.

We spent too much time in surf and skate shops where my brother wanted to hang out. We spent too much time in beachy boutiques with pink and purple tube tops I would never ever wear. And we spent too much time on the beach when I would have rather been reading in the hotel.

I was reading *Anna Karenina* at the time (who was arguably punished as violently by Tolstoy as Emma Bovary was by Flaubert) and spent at least three days straight lying on the beach reading it.

My mother couldn't stomach it. Every time I opened the book, she was visibly irritated. I can understand now that my retreat from the beach activities or from our family banter undermined her expectations of what a spring break family vacation should be, and if the vacation wasn't all "fun in the sun" we might remember that our family was struggling to the point where there was little money for college, no savings for anything else, and soon there would be no house to return to from the vacations we couldn't afford.

But she never said anything like that. Instead, she kept pronouncing the same warning with a sort of moral authority: if you keep reading *that* book, your face will not tan evenly.

What my mom didn't know: I had read my Didion. I was taking notes. And my mother urging me to put away that book, *Anna Karenina*, because it was causing an uneven tan would become the opening scene in my college essay—the one that helped land me a scholarship and get me to New York.

New York was, as promised, where I finally felt like I belonged. Until, a long decade later, I found myself crying, not in Didion's laundromats but in the stairwell of my loft in Brooklyn and in the elevator of the art magazine where I worked in Midtown. And Didion too gave me the remedy for the feeling of staying too long at the fair: Los Angeles.

ENDNOTES:

1. Joan Didion, "Goodbye to All That," in *Slouching Towards Bethlehem* (New York: Farrar, Straus and Giroux, 1968), 236.
2. Joan Didion, "On Keeping a Notebook," in *Slouching Towards Bethlehem* (New York: Farrar, Straus and Giroux, 1968), 140.
3. Didion, "On Keeping a Notebook," 140.
4. Didion, "On Keeping a Notebook," 133.

Dark Mirror:
Reflections on the Golden Dream

By Steffie Nelson

"THIS IS A STORY about love and death in the golden land, and begins with the country."[1]

Those words, the first sentence of the first essay in Joan Didion's *Slouching Towards Bethlehem*, struck me as vividly as the sunshine-yellow and Day-Glo-orange cover I found tucked into my mother's bookshelf one summer after college. I was an aspiring magazine journalist with a creative writing degree, but Didion had eluded me until that moment, like so many things that don't appear until we're ready for them. I'd studied Yeats, though, and I recognized the nod to his poem "The Second Coming," in which a sphinxlike beast turns its "blank and pitiless"[2] gaze, and slowly moves its thighs…

So it was actually the Irish poet—and the acid hues of that 1979 edition, which currently sits on *my* bookshelf—that led me to the woman whose writing lit up some nerve center in me, speaking to me in a language I'd never heard before, about a California where the sun's gaze was as pitiless as a beast's. Somehow I didn't

21

read futility in her words; I felt desire, and a willingness to risk everything for the prize. Teetering on the edge of adulthood, it was as if I'd been handed a psychic map pointing west.

Love. Death. The golden land. The country.

That opening line of "Some Dreamers of the Golden Dream" is so simple yet so loaded with meaning, it's almost a mantra. It reveals nothing but promises everything, and puts us in the driver's seat—because in a flash, epic crimes and passions and landscapes unfurl like teaser reels across our minds. You might even call it lazy, leaning as it does on the reader's imagination, but that's the territory of the essay, anyway: the chasm between the glittering projection and what pans out. We'd like to believe that the dream will send us directly over the rainbow, reinvented and renewed, with pockets full of shiny nuggets and a suntan, too. But of course, the odds are against us. In this land, despair is bred at the same rate as hope, and Didion places her bets on the former. In fact, when this essay was originally published in the *Saturday Evening Post* in 1966, it was titled "How Can I Tell Them There's Nothing Left?"

On the surface the tale of a marriage gone sour, an illicit affair, and a murder, Didion frames this exurban tragedy as the Golden Dream running its inevitable course and, in so doing, flips the narrative so that the dream is more defined by its end than its beginning. Without the flameout (in this case Lucille Miller's literal incineration of her husband, Gordon, in the passenger seat of their Volkswagen in San Bernardino), we only know half the story.

"Of course she came from somewhere else," we are told about the thirty-five-year-old mother of a teenage daughter, "for this is a Southern California story."[3] From the start, it's obvious that nothing good can happen in this place just an hour east of Los Angeles, where the winds blow hot and women cobble their aspirations from movies, newspapers, and the radio. According to her father, Lucille Miller "wanted to see the world."[4] In this setup that was her fatal flaw.

What she did get to see was the one-acre lot through her picture window, and it wasn't enough. Didion visited the California Institution for Women at Frontera, where Miller was incarcerated after being convicted of murder in the first degree, and found it to be populated by "murderesses...girls who somehow misunderstood the promise."[5] This was already clear about Miller, she implies, from the high lacquered hairdo she'd worn in the courtroom: as ready for her close-up as Norma Desmond ever was.

Didion shows no compassion for Lucille Miller, but I find it hard not to pity this woman who was self-aware enough to realize that she'd settled for a life that would never fulfill her, and foolish and corrupt enough to think she could change her fate by burning her husband alive—an idea that came to her after watching *Double Indemnity*. The question is, when and where did the schism happen? Recounting the boilerplate B-movie dialogue exchanged by Miller and her lover, who'd promptly abandoned her once she was accused of murder, Didion asserts, "the dream was teaching the dreamers how to live."[6] But was it fiction dictating the script, or was this the glass Didion herself was looking through?

She's such a master at manipulating the tension between utopia and dystopia that many LA writers—most of us from somewhere else, too—have internalized this queasy balance as our geographic destiny. But I've lived in Los Angeles for more than a decade, and I still don't know if I've been to that pitiless place. I believe I've shielded my eyes against the same slanting sun and heard the Santa Anas rustling through the eucalyptus like snakes, but are those actual memories or just impressions left by language? They are like phantom experiences, in which sensations exist without physical cause.

"The future always looks good in the golden land, because no one remembers the past,"[7] Didion famously claimed in this essay. However, looking at the now iconic portraits of the young writer, I see a woman who is reluctant to smile for the camera, as if happiness or hope were somehow naive, given all that she knows. By any account she actually *was* living the dream during this time, but the passionate gratitude her fans have for Joan the person can be explained, I think, by our certainty that she never bought into the myth. She had seen the world and accurately gauged its promise. And then she made her place in the sun anyway—defying her own odds. There she will remain, plain and uncompromising, arms crossed—nobody's fool, nobody's victim. The fact that her darkest human dread was borne out, decades later, makes her youthful vigilance seem that much more exacting.

I've often wondered whether Didion, an avowed atheist who has stated her belief in "geology" over a personal God, knew about Yeats's dedication to mysticism and the occult when she borrowed the title of her collection from him. His language brilliantly lends itself to the explosive creativity and chaos of the late 1960s—like the "sages standing in God's holy fire"[8] from his second most famous poem, "Sailing to Byzantium"—but "The Second Coming" also alludes to a pagan awakening that definitely suits the era but may not have suited Joan. Still, I'd like to think that somewhere within her solemn heart—maybe in the part of her that walked onto airplanes barefoot and gave her daughter the impossible, romantic name of Quintana Roo—she found space for a golden dream to drift in, and a center that would hold.

ENDNOTES:

1. Joan Didion, "Some Dreamers of the Golden Dream," in *Slouching Towards Bethlehem* (New York: Farrar, Straus and Giroux, 1968), 3.
2. William Butler Yeats, "The Second Coming," in *Collected Poems* (New York: MacMillan, 1924).
3. Didion, "Some Dreamers of the Golden Dream," 7.
4. Didion, "Some Dreamers of the Golden Dream," 7.
5. Didion, "Some Dreamers of the Golden Dream," 25.
6. Didion, "Some Dreamers of the Golden Dream," 17.
7. Didion, "Some Dreamers of the Golden Dream," 4.
8. William Butler Yeats, "Sailing to Byzantium," in *Collected Poems* (New York: MacMillan, 1924).

At This Precise Intersection of Time and Space:

A Response to Joan Didion's "At the Dam"

By Margaret Wappler

SINCE THE AUGUST AFTERNOON of 2002 when I first drove past the Hoover Dam, the oppressive heat surrounding the structure has never entirely left my skin or my psyche. The killer heat of the West—it almost got me. In a way I wouldn't see for a long time, the West did lay claim to a few things. And the remembrance of those things will slip into a day when I'm not looking, not thinking, like a pall. Driving up to the dam— the heat socking into the truck, the desert a dun-colored stain in all directions, my life about to rip itself fresh—was the first stage of my rebirth into Los Angeles, the West, as an anxious, hopeful creature.

On the first day of our cross-country move from Chicago to Los Angeles, everything was a blur, with a few exceptions. The flats of Texas where we saw lightning jag from its cloudy nest down to the ground. Flagstaff, Arizona, where we stopped for the night and ate shrimp and drank blue margaritas in a carpeted hotel dining room so cold it was almost refrigerated.

The next day plunged us into the desert. The insufferable heat was an air trap, waiting outside of our U-Haul. We were vibrating across Highway 93 with everything we owned, living and inanimate, inside the truck. Outside the temperature was 103 degrees. We were running out of gas. There was nothing in the desert. I didn't understand what was happening. Where were all the features? How long could *not much of anything* go on? Where were the living things? Were we going to break down in this truck with our cat, Lima, who kept slinking from the front to the back, and then underneath the brake pad? Would we all go wandering in the desert for help, never to be seen again? Would we look like those cartoons of gaunt near carcasses crawling through the endless sands, whispering "water, water"? Would we die out here? Would the West be inhospitable to two Midwestern art kids drawn to it by the cracked moonstone mysticism of Fleetwood Mac and P. T. Anderson, who somehow captured the true romantic nature of a 99-Cent Store at night?

"It's going to be okay," Adam said when I panicked about making it to the next gas station. A sign had flashed at some point saying, "Gas station, a million miles away," and we had flagrantly ignored it. The empty tank sign had been on for several miles. We were on a detour from the reliable straights of Interstate 40, rattling toward the Hoover Dam, the gateway from the Wild West to what was west of that, the end of the continent. Neither of us had ever laid eyes on the dam. Really, Adam wanted to see it and I wanted to make him happy in this small way. But as we drew closer to it, everything felt worse.

I was still swallowing tears from saying goodbye to Lizzie, my almost sister, and Chris, a guy I accidentally fell in love with.

Goodbye to Chicago, goodbye to our house with the checkered floor, goodbye to the nights I had spent riding my bike to a dive bar with Chris after work, him looking back at me and kicking out his foot in a wave, goodbye to all that. I was headed west to transform into a better writer and a better wife—two jobs I had assigned myself, one with an overblown sense of destiny, the other out of love and duty. But I was chafing against my uniform. I worried I was fundamentally unfit for this type of women's work.

Maybe California would save me, would save us. Maybe on the fifth sunset, according to some legend as of yet unknown, I'd find peace as simply and efficiently as changing four lanes, merging, merging, merging in one fluid movement. I'd eat a Meyer lemon from our tree in our new backyard and taste the kind of clean grace that can wipe memory. I'd write a book where palm trees talked and wake up next to this person, feeling right.

As we got closer to the dam, the air-conditioning sputtered out. The truck, on its apocalyptic diet of gasoline fumes, hurtled forward seemingly out of sheer physics. Anxiety tightened the screws holding up my neck, raked down my back in burning rushes.

I never expected to be struck by an engineering marvel. In fact, I've probably said the phrase "engineering marvel" only a few times in my life, but when we drove past it, everything else occupying my mind was blotted out. The desert of Black Canyon erupted into a mammoth half-bowl, a curve of concrete 726 feet tall that can be seen from space, separating the head of Lake Mead from the blue neck of the Colorado River. From our vantage point on the highway, scant yards away, it rose out of nothing like a religious monument. An altar to human ingenuity and the belief that it will always save us, from nature, from an indifferent God. The missionary fever of the dam's construction, which had cost ninety-six men their lives, not to mention one dog who was crushed by a truck. How many other people and animals had lost their lives to it in secret ways? In ways that amount to quiet devastation—a body broken, worked to destruction, so that it could erect an engineered body that nature supposedly couldn't destroy? Could our belief in progress exist without tossing human lives into its open maw? And is this always the way progress happens, with blood and plaques and tourists later?

Now that we had passed it, saying nothing more than the occasional obscenity, only slowing down because we couldn't afford to stop, our circumstances seemed worse than ever. We had to keep driving. Driving till we did find the gas station with seconds to spare. And now that we were safe, our truck satiated with the fossil fuels it needed to go on, I was glad, in a grim kind of way, to have seen it. There was no turning back now. I had to accept my decision to restart our life together, with all of its unforeseen consequences.

Replenished with gas, the air-conditioning attacked with renewed vigor, beating back the ancient heat until the city rolled into view, first as the straight tentacles that shoot out around San Bernardino and then eventually as bougainvillea and taco stands and signs bleached by sun. The day we drove in, we drove straight into Sunset Junction, a giant music festival on Sunset Boulevard, like the city was throwing us a welcoming party. At the sight of the peach-colored sun sinking behind a young drunken crowd, I was euphoric. We had made it. We had survived our first gauntlet by breaching the West! And here was a lusty bacchanalia to herald our arrival! We slipped into the crowd, becoming a part of the city, a seamless and beautiful communion. It wouldn't always be this easy, starting over. I learned to cling to those alighted moments, each one a lifeboat in a choppy sea.

Ten years later, everything living or loved in that truck would be changed or dead. The relationship—gone. Lima the cat—dead. That antique lamp I carefully packed into a box with pillows to cushion its every blow—in the dumpster. These are the carcasses of progress; I remember their suffering but the world is indifferent. Some symbols of progress, like the Hoover Dam, demand that we look at it and pray to it loudly, as tourists, as children passing into the West. But there are shrines everywhere, your own private ones, that hear your silent prayers, too. At midnight, you allow yourself to acknowledge the destruction you ravaged to build something new, something that would do what you wanted. Remains still poke out from the bloodstained soil. But above the dirt, you have constructed something high functioning, maybe even glorious. During the day, we all agree to call our own shrines marvels of engineering. They are the spoils of progress, and testimonies to all we can do. We bend the forces of nature, of fate, to our wills. At the Hoover Dam, we are grateful for every precious drop of water it sends down a path we forged for us.

We Dream of the Cloverleaf

By Jessica Hundley

JOAN DIDION IS FASCINATED by the freeway, by the hypnotic sprawl of LA pavement. In her essay, "Bureaucrats," published in *The White Album*, she describes the meditative rhythm of the lane change, the need for "total surrender, a concentration so intense as to seem a kind of narcosis." In what feels like an ecstatic proclamation, she describes the freeway system as Los Angeles's "only secular communion."[1]

I come from a place of cow paths mutated to asphalt, where long-ago bovine whimsy dictates direction. I come from a place of pockmarked country roads lined with piles of ancient stone, rocks tattooed by the sweat of century-dead Yankee farmers.

Where I'm from, a "street" is a place lined with salt-stained siding, sprinkler hiss, and lawnmower drone guarding never-used front entries, kids in the back and mom opening the side screen door to shake out crumbs from the tablecloth. At night, headlights carve close through blackness and echo, across darkened leaf.

But here...

Here, the way is free and the sky is open.

Here—in Didion's Los Angeles—the city is shoelaced together—its farthest edges pulled up and close by a thin and graceful ribbon of pavement. The road here is long and true, it shoots arrows of cement through clusters of adobe and palm, burrows under humped mounds of dirt and deer grass to emerge back again into a bleached daylight. It swoops down, around and over, a hawk's path through smog and jasmine.

Here, we dream of the cloverleaf. We look down from the tin-can airplane, homesick for the grid.

I think of Didion's secular communion. Didion caressing the 405 in her 1969 Daytona Yellow T-top Corvette Stingray, wearing something long and silk and flowing, a cigarette pressed between lips. Didion in total surrender, her mind clean, her eyes clear and filled with a sublime reverence.

It was Didion's Los Angeles that called me west. Didion's Los Angeles, in the time before the screens. Before the barrage. Before the bits and the pixels and the data.

The communion then was just you and your machine. You, alone inside your glistening steel husk, gliding over the shimmer of rising heat. Vinyl licking the curve beneath the knee. The glare of Pacific hovering over hood. The head empty, the windows down—the only sound, engine whine under the static of AM radio. "All the leaves are brown," The Mamas and The Papas sing, as you fly through the blue-green blur of California.

Today, the rapture is numbed by the digital. The disconnect never complete, the cord never cut. Stuck fast, unmoving, the pavement turned to quicksand, we wait out traffic with distraction. Our lips flutter into microphone, speakers beat deep in our guts, and our minds are full to bursting.

The communion is still there, yes. Our highway, the great unifier. Together we stand, united we drive.

An actress stabs the lid with mascara, late for an audition. The Santa Anas blow bits of yellowed grass from the back of a gardener's truck. An exec worries over his hairline, while in another car beside him a woman sits alone and weeps, chest shuddering, her cries drowned out by the blast of the air conditioner.

And sometimes, on the rare days when clogged arteries give way to flow, when the sun glows Daytona Yellow over a clear, clean line of moving cars, the rapture returns too.

I put the top down. I turn the volume up. "All the leaves are brown," it sings. I press the pedal gently to the floor. I glide. I caress. There is no resistance. No hesitation. Everything goes perfectly blank, the asphalt beneath me now a golden thread from the spinning wheel. Empty, elated, wind hot on the skin, I worship.

I kneel, to the holy trinity of car and road and California.

And I think of Didion. Of the self-possessed woman, hands light on the wheel, turning into the curve with elegance and intuition. Of Didion, wearing something long and flowing, cigarette to lips, mind clean, as she surrenders to the moment, to herself.

I think of Didion, calling me west, calling me HERE—to where the sky is open and the way is free.

ENDNOTES:

1. Joan Didion, "Bureaucrats," in *The White Album* (New York: Simon & Schuster, 1979), 83.

Long Ride Home

By Christine Lennon

ON THE BACK WALL in our tiny powder room hangs a print of a Julian Wasser photograph of Joan Didion. It's one of the iconic series from 1970 taken outside of Didion and her husband John Gregory Dunne's home on Franklin Avenue in Hollywood. In the photograph she wears a long jersey dress and lights a cigarette while leaning against her Corvette Stingray. I placed this image there deliberately, so that anyone who's intrigued by it can take the time to admire it alone, without distraction.

I have looked at this picture so many times that I feel like I could step into the frame. I can sense the rough driveway under my shoes and smell the smoke and sulfur from the lit match, and the scent of jasmine that she always noticed, which is heavy in the air all over Los Angeles. The garage doors in the background of the photo have two rectangular windows that, to me, look like watchful eyes. The overgrown bushes above them have become raised eyebrows. It's like the garage is so in awe of this person with her lank, messy hair and brazenly sexy car that it can't look away.

The photo was a wedding present from my husband, in 2005, and it was in lieu of a sparkly ring. We had eloped and skipped over the engagement portion of the proceedings entirely—no diamond required. The gift was his way of telling me that he really knew me, expressing both that he understood that I would like this picture more than a ring, and that he had Didion to thank for luring me to Los Angeles.

I devoured Didion's essays for the first time when I was twenty-three and trying to find my way in New York. I moved to "The City" from Florida and stumbled into a career writing for fashion magazines, so, naturally, Joan Didion—who has become the patron saint of so many young women who move to New York to write—became my spirit guide. She was a fellow outsider who had infiltrated a glamorous place like *Vogue*, and many of her personal stories from that era of her life as a young, single, and somewhat clueless junior reporter, functioned as a kind of guidebook. From what I could tell, she survived in that culture because she worked very hard, sat very still, and hoped no one would notice that she didn't belong there. I adopted the same strategy, and eventually landed at *Vogue* myself for a year in between stints at *Harper's Bazaar*. Like any decent writer trained in the parlance of fashion magazines, Didion hoovered the details of what made a person, or a life, fashionable. She could identify the "right" skirt length at a hundred paces. She knew how to tie a scarf around her neck just so, and that a square cut made an emerald fashionable. I imagine she hoped that kind of information would protect her, that it was like holding the answer key for a chic life. And so did I.

For ten years, I shared her deep love of New York and the belief that "something extraordinary would happen, any minute, any day, any month,"[1] as she wrote in the closing essay of

Slouching Towards Bethlehem, "Goodbye to All That." Then, just like Joan, I soured on the whole experience. I started questioning everything, including my desk job and my shaky marriage. I visited Los Angeles from New York a few times for work and my view of the city was confined to the Chateau Marmont and the back seat of a black town car that would shuttle me to meet with various advertisers and interviews. At first, I didn't get it. Then in the spring of 2001, I ventured out to the desert for the first time, driving past the windmills into that rocky lunar landscape, and I was hooked. Los Angeles may confound others, but it was, suddenly, the only place that made any sense to me. I moved out of my apartment. I went back to Didion's essays. And then I discovered Maria Wyeth and her yellow Corvette in *Play It As It Lays,* Didion's second novel that was published in 1970, the year I was born. Yes, Maria was morbid, depressed, and desperately self-involved. There were mental hospitals, drug overdoses, and a mother devoured by a pack of coyotes in the barren desert wasteland. It wasn't exactly endorsed by the LA Chamber of Commerce. It didn't matter. I related to her uncertainty, her jaded worldview, and that anxious need to get behind the wheel of a car with no destination in mind. Eighteen months later, at thirty-two, I left Manhattan with only divorce papers, a few suitcases of clothes, a stack of magazine clips, and enough money in my savings account to start over.

The thought of speeding across the plains and through that dry expanse of desert to a shiny city at the edge of the continent thrilled me. Riding public transportation in New York was passive and often aggravating. Driving your own car was about freedom and control. In Didion's book, the way Maria prowled the streets of Hollywood, looping around the vast city for hours every day and letting her hair tangle in the wind, felt just dangerous enough to be appealing. Of course, the car I was driving was a profoundly sensible Volkswagen Passat. (A Passat and a Stingray are both cars in the way a mole and a gazelle are both animals.) But I didn't care. In my mind, I was fleeing the bad vibes of a failed marriage in a yellow sports car, just like Maria. It took me four days to make it to LA on a meandering route through Nashville, Austin, and Phoenix. When I finally pulled into town on the 10, I felt like it was the end of a movie, and I was my own hero walking into the sunset. I was free.

I met my second, current, (hopefully *final*) husband six months after I moved here, at a sad bar on Melrose, when reality had started to settle in. I was working as a magazine journalist, but the Hollywood I experienced was carefully managed by publicists. My days weren't spent chronicling a cultural revolution. Instead, I interviewed celebrities over expensive, sparse, and mannered lunches. Didion's version of the city, a moody, paranoid, soulless but somehow darkly romantic place, where you spent your evenings at louche dinner parties hosted in rambling houses in sketchy neighborhoods and "spotted minor actresses"[2] at the gynecologist's office, still existed, in a way. But it was fading fast.

Now, sixteen years later, it has almost completely vanished. Yes, there are still plenty of C-list actors, but they're all hiding from smartphones in private clubs and either using the back entrance at the clinic or paying the doctor to make house calls. Don't get me wrong, I love it here. But I do not love driving here. Over the last fifty years, the city's population has swollen by over a million people. Who knows how many more cars are on the road? Driving in Los Angeles is nothing like it was then, when Maria could cross over four lanes of freeway traffic without braking. Didion writes of this with poetic grace:

"She drove it as a riverman runs a river, every day more attuned to its currents, its deceptions…Again and again she returned to an intricate stretch just south of the interchange where successful passage from the Hollywood onto the Harbor required a diagonal move across four lanes of traffic. On the afternoon she finally did it without once braking or once losing the beat on the radio she was exhilarated, and that night slept dreamlessly."[3]

Reading this makes the palm-lined avenues and looping interchanges seem like a cruel temptation. When I'm in my car, I sit mostly idle, grinding my brake pads and back molars into nubs. My speedometer registers twenty-five miles, thirty miles on a good day. I creep along, watching the endless snake of red taillights stretch out before me.

Still, I think of Didion when I drive, now in my sturdy Volvo with its very un-Stingray third row of seats to fit the carpool crowd. I pass those same street signs on the 101 that haunted Maria's dreams when I drive my children to school in the morning.

"Maria lay at night in the still of Beverly Hills and saw the great signs soar overhead at seventy miles an hour, *Normandie ¼ Vermont 3/4, Harbor Fwy 1.*"[4]

It's funny that LA traffic is responsible for my only brush with my hero. In November of 2005, my husband and I went to the Hammer Museum to hear Didion read from *The Year of Magical Thinking* to a crowd so huge that several hundred people had to listen over speakers outside in the courtyard. We were late. The brutal slog to Westwood from our old house near Hollywood, where the Wasser photograph had been hanging for only five months, took us even longer than usual. In *Magical Thinking*,

Didion mentions that there are certain streets in town that she can't let herself explore because it would be too painful to relive those memories of her younger life, with her husband and young daughter. And she writes about how the three of them would drive into Beverly Hills from their home on Portuguese Bend in Palos Verdes for dinner. It seems almost laughable now, thinking that anyone would attempt that drive on a school night voluntarily.

Eventually, we found a parking space and sprinted to the museum. We rushed into an elevator to get to the auditorium upstairs just as the doors were closing. At first, we thought we were alone. But I felt the prickle of heat on my neck and knew that there were eyes on me from behind. I turned around to see Joan Didion standing in the corner, by herself. She was impossibly tiny, pressed against the steel wall behind her and gripping the handrail. Her presence, however, was huge. She was boring holes into me with her intense stare, and my eyes locked with hers, those limpid eyes that noticed everything. She was wearing an ivory silk blouse under a black jacket, with a heavy shoulder bag that she would later take with her onstage when she read to the crowd. I wasn't entirely sure she was real. It felt like I was seeing a ghost, in keeping with the theme of the book and the evening. When I looked over at my husband and saw him looking at her looking at me, with his jaw slightly agape, I knew she was real. I stood there in stunned silence like an idiot. I mentioned that I make a living interviewing famous people, but nothing prepared me for this. I was motionless and dumbstruck, just as awed by her presence as those garage doors, unable to offer even the feeblest compliment.

"I love your work" just wasn't enough.

What I didn't know at the time was that Quintana Roo, her daughter, had passed away just before the book went to press, and she refused to make changes to the manuscript to reflect that. If I had to guess why she was staring at me so intently, I suspect that because she wasn't wearing her glasses, my general presence—a tall blonde with similar facial features, around the same age her daughter was when she died—reminded her of her daughter, and it was hard for her to look away. It was like she was seeing a ghost, too.

I haven't had a cigarette in a very long time, and I've never been cool enough to drive a Corvette. Somehow, I understand that Wasser photograph anyway. When I drive through the streets that she knew so well, dressed (unintentionally) like Maria in my own "cotton skirt, a jersey, sandals she could kick off when she wanted the touch of the accelerator,"[5] with hastily brushed hair, noticing the smell of the air and the feel of heat on my skin, her words and observations ride along with me. She's the closest thing I have to a copilot. (Should I make a bumper sticker?)

When I followed my curiosity about Didion and driving into a deep search on the Internet, I learned that when she and her family moved to Brentwood from Malibu, Didion traded in her Stingray for a Volvo. I'll admit that I found this deeply satisfying. It does make me wonder if the Corvette is still on the road, lovingly preserved by its owner the way Didion fans like me cherish her words. On the days when I make it out of the city and break through the stop-and-go traffic, I still hope to see it in its Daytona Yellow glory, like it just launched itself out of the frame of the photo to cross four lanes of the freeway in front me. And I remember to roll down the windows and enjoy the ride.

ENDNOTES:

1. Joan Didion, "Goodbye to All That," in *Slouching Towards Bethlehem* (New York: Farrar, Straus and Giroux, 1968), 229.
2. Joan Didion, "Why I Write," *The New York Times,* December 5, 1976, https://www.nytimes.com/1976/12/05/archives/why-i-write-why-i-write.html
3. Joan Didion, *Play It As It Lays* (New York: Farrar, Straus and Giroux, 1970), 16.
4. Didion, *Play It As It Lays,* 16.
5. Didion, *Play It As It Lays,* 15.

That Was a Very Pretty Image:
On the Joan Didion Fragility Myth

By Catherine Wagley

I'VE ALWAYS LIKED THE same photos that everyone else does, of Joan Didion in big sunglasses and long dresses; of her windswept hair, while she stands by the beach with a cigarette in one hand, a whiskey glass balancing on a deck railing beside her. They are, undeniably, seductive. But these images have, over time, done what such images have done to other smart, feminine women who pose too often for photographs. They've allowed us to treat her slight figure and nice clothes as primary, her craft as a confounding, mystique-building coincidence that we can marvel at just as we marvel at her image. After the fashion brand Celine launched its Didion ad in 2015, featuring the eighty-year-old writer with her signature bob and dark glasses looking frail but, again, composed, her fragility graduated fully into mainstream branding. *Elle* magazine described her "minimalist" style as "at once fragile and strong,"[1] and fashion blogs ran pieces celebrating Didion's pull and influence over other women, as if it were her distinct, intrinsic ability to be wispy and smart, rather than something more wrought and deliberate, that compelled us all.

Didion was a visiting Regents' Lecturer at Berkeley in 1975— her own former professors had invited her, still hoping she would abandon magazine writing for serious scholarship—and she made something of a stir. Caitlin Flanagan wrote about this in *The Atlantic* in 2012, as part of her often condescending review of Didion's 2011 memoir, *Blue Nights*. Flanagan, then fourteen and daughter of Berkeley professor Thomas Flanagan, describes women hanging around Didion's office and lingering along her route to catch a glimpse. "There's something *weird* going on with Joan Didion and women,"[2] Flanagan's father commented at the time.

As Didion prepared to lecture on campus, her husband, the writer John Gregory Dunne, came up to visit from LA. Didion and Dunne went together to see the room that Heidi, the Berkeley English Department's secretary, had chosen for Didion's talk. "It's too small," said Dunne. Didion agreed. Heidi, her last name lost to the annals, felt snubbed and booked the biggest lecture hall available—hardly fillable. But people, mostly "tearful women" in Flanagan's words, were turned away. Didion, who came off as socially anxious and delicate at faculty dinners, demonstrated fierce pull over women in particular. "She gave us quiet days in Malibu and flowers in our hair," wrote Flanagan, and "a way of being female and being writers that no one else could give."[3]

This isn't wrong. When I first encountered Didion, I too identified something I wanted: through her descriptions of flowers, drapes, headaches, and anxieties she insisted that a writer could acknowledge femininity and vulnerability while still being incisively competent. She intentionally made her situation—and her white female privilege, to the extent that she understood it—transparent as she cut into questions of politics and grappled with cultural shifts. But the way she crafted that transparency to serve her purposes has led both to deserved criticisms and misreadings, largely because we still struggle to reconcile what she did and said with how she looked and felt; she is called a "femme fatale," "shrinking," "elitist," "cold." Don Bachardy, the painter and socialite, called her clammy and a climber.[4] In a 1979 profile, *The New York Times* book critic Michiko Kakutani described Didion, who agonized over pleats in the dining room curtains during their first meeting, as resembling a character in Didion's own 1977 novel *A Book of Common Prayer*, with her "extreme and volatile thinness."[5] Another friend, trying to reconcile the writer's edge with her quietness back in the 1970s, called her "a fragile, little stainless steel machine."[6] While pushback against this image of the writer's fashionable delicateness has also grown—Michelle Dean addressed Didion's edge in her 2018 book *Sharp,* and Deborah Nelson's 2017 *Tough Enough* unpacked her "emotional hardness"[7]—countless interviews with Didion since the 1970s have addressed her delicacy in some form or another. For instance, when Charlie Rose, still twenty-two years from his #metoo reckoning, had her on his show in 1996, he tried to articulate his surprise at her unforgiving prose, saying, "You don't look like a killer…[you're] eighty-eight pounds of…"[8]

Interviewing her for the *Paris Review* in 1978, Linda Kuehl asked Didion, "How did the 'fragility of Joan Didion' myth start?"[9]

"Because I'm small,"[10] Didion said, then also cited her quietness and tendency to let sentences drift off. She had written something similar in the preface to her 1968 collection *Slouching Towards Bethlehem*, acknowledging the role her physical smallness and "neurotically inarticulate"[11] disposition played in compelling people to trust her. Her tendency to fold her uncertainty into writing fed the myth too, even if the writing itself was far from uncertain.

Didion's 1972 essay on the Women's Movement, first published in *The New York Times*, offers odd, telling insight into her own relationship to both weakness and style. She is angry in this essay, about a number of things, including the didacticism of second wave feminism and the way the mainstream press has presented it, as if the goal is self-expression and fulfillment, or reading Latin classics in gazebos. "Fewer diapers, more Dante," quips Didion. "That was a very pretty image."[12] And a packageable one. The female experience she wanted to acknowledge could not so easily be sold, as it incorporated what she called "irreconcilable difference,"[13] ambivalence mixed in with conviction and a feeling of being at once in touch with and confounded by the world surrounding her. Other women of Didion's generation also suspected 1970s feminism of peddling too clear-cut and aspirational a reality (Aya Tarlow, Penny Slinger, Simone Forti, writers and artists who embraced 1960s liberation and lived outside the conventions of traditional femininity but found "feminist" too rigid a definition), but Didion pilloried its rhetoric with particular venom, excoriating its lack of vulnerability and contradictions in writing that itself left very little room for those things.

Later, Didion would become much better at conveying irreconcilable difference and doing so with such diligence that complication could not be mistaken for confusion. In the political writing she did for the *New York Review of Books* in the late 1980s and 1990s, well after the glow of her first two essay collections faded, she used her powers of observation more like a scalpel. She dissected the specialized language of "the democratic process" and the way politicians used such specialization to make their trade even more elitist; she found in the storytelling by officials and media about the attack on the Central Park Jogger a sinister, romantically capitalist notion of New York, one into which a young female jogger who works on Wall Street fits but five teenagers of color do not. The jogger, "handsome and pretty and educated and white"[14] (as Didion called her, quoting *The New York Times*), had the kind of privilege Didion also had. The jogger was treated as too vulnerable to speak or to have her name spoken, a fetishization based on the assumption, Didion argued, that rape victims should and do feel shame at their feminine fragility and violation. This premise, and the desire for New York City to be a haven for only a certain brand of attractive, educated white person, led in part to the bungled case that Didion condemned twelve years before the exoneration of the Central Park Five.

One night in Oregon in 1992, Didion and her husband, John Dunne, spoke back-to-back as part of the Portland Arts and Lectures Series. Dunne went first, talking in a self-aggrandizing way about his feelings about truth-telling, poking at his wife's neuroses occasionally, mentioning her obsessively detailed archive of recipes and her blueprint for her own funeral (she'd included "a specific injunction not to use the twenty-third psalm," said Dunne, calling it "passive crap"). Before he stepped down to give Didion the stage, he told audience members not to be alarmed if he dashed up to pat her on the back. "It's not wife abuse," he said, adding that she had a bad flu. She'd been portrayed as neurotic as well as ailing by the time she took the mic.[15]

As soon as she started talking, however, the atmosphere changed. She did not mention her flu, and dug right into the details of the story she wanted to tell, about women whose narratives did not fit streamlined, mainstream narratives, about the way politicians and journalists used these women as pawns, about a writer's obligation to truth even when it must be excavated, and about the spuriousness of objectivity. The neuroses pinned on her minutes before disappeared in her fierce clarity. Didion's desire to make room for uncertainty in her own story and others, so often mistaken for evidence of her glamorous infirmity, was actually part of a lifelong commitment to carving out clear, accurate space for messier realities—human fragility among them.

ENDNOTES:

1. Justine Carreon, "Six Outfits Inspired by Joan Didion," *Elle*, January 7, 2015, https://www.elle.com/fashion/shopping/how-to/g9656/outfits-inspired-by-joan-didion/

2. Caitlin Flanagan, "The Autumn of Joan Didion," *The Atlantic*, January/February 2012, https://www.theatlantic.com/magazine/archive/2012/01/the-autumn-of-joan-didion/308851/.

3. Flanagan, "The Autumn of Joan Didion."

4. Lili Anolik, "How Joan Didion the Writer Became Joan Didion the Legend," *Vanity Fair*, February 2, 2016, https://www.vanityfair.com/culture/2016/02/joan-didion-writer-los-angeles.

5. Michiko Kakutani, "Joan Didion: Staking Out California," *The New York Times*, June 10, 1979, https://www.nytimes.com/1979/06/10/books/didion-calif.html.

6. Kakutani, "Joan Didion."

7. Deborah Nelson, *Tough Enough: Arbus, Arendt, Didion, McCarthy, Sontag, Weil* (Chicago: University of Chicago Press, 2017), 172.

8. *Charlie Rose*, PBS September 17, 1996, in broadcast syndication.

9. Linda Kuehl, "Joan Didion, The Art of Fiction No. 71," *The Paris Review*, Issue 74, Fall-Winter 1978, https://www.theparisreview.org/interviews/3439/joan-didion-the-art-of-fiction-no-71-joan-didion.

10. Linda Kuehl, "Joan Didion, The Art of Fiction No. 71."

11. Joan Didion, *Slouching Toward Bethlehem* (New York: Farrar, Straus and Giroux, 1968/1990), xvi.

12. Joan Didion, "The Women's Movement," in *The White Album* (New York: Simon & Schuster, 1979), 109.

13. Didion, *The White Album*, 117.

14. Joan Didion, "Sentimental Journeys," *The New York Review of Books*, January 17, 1991, https://www.nybooks.com/articles/1991/01/17/new-york-sentimental-journeys/.

15. Joan Didion and John Dunne, Sept. 23, 1992, Portland Literary Arts, Portland, Oregon, MP3, 52:45, https://literary-arts.org/?powerpress_pinw=9913-literary-arts-archive.

Despair and Doing

By Su Wu

THERE WERE DAYS IN the desert when I would lie motionless staring at the shadows of the mesquite tree in the courtyard of his home, which he'd built himself on a piece of inhospitable land over the course of two years that he would never get back. The courtyard was long and shingled in redwood and had a space jutting off one side, and I asked him once about it, why he'd built this awkwardly shaped room that collected wood scraps and sucked in old projects, and he said it was not a room, it was the sky. He said he wanted to look up and see the entire Milky Way. These were the days before I began to wear on him. I was useless in the face of real talent and this rural life; I could not bake nor sew nor save up for a rainy day nor even entertain myself, but I would recite poetry out of the blue at dinner until one day he snapped at me for interrupting his thoughts. All he wanted to do after dark was drink. Some days, maybe as the sun was setting and feeling a sudden rush of wherewithal, I would get up from bed and write, and some days there was even one line or two of a poem.

Feel bad: because it's true
Feel bad: because there's nothing new

Then I would sleep until it got too hot to sleep anymore. When, in that first geographical paragraph of "Some Dreamers of the Golden Dream" Joan Didion described the "harsher California, haunted by the Mojave just beyond the mountains, devastated by the hot dry Santa Ana wind that comes down through the passes at a hundred miles an hour and whines through the Eucalyptus windbreaks and works on the nerves,"[1] she was not writing about where I lived. I was living in the place that did the haunting, beyond the mountains. I would hear the studio working and his assistants grinding stone in a whir of productivity, and would look in the fridge for a cold Coca-Cola, which is also what Didion had for breakfast every morning. Other days I was up at dawn, and the day had promise, and I started another project I would never finish, and other days I had an assignment, and so I finished a project that didn't matter at all but because I thought of myself as somewhat reliable. Maybe I didn't know at the time I was depressed, but I am not so sure in retrospect either. I could have just been dehydrated. I know that the day would drag on while I tried to find a reason for it. I know nothing felt worth doing, but everything hurt. It hurt like no one had ever hurt before, and in an inconsequential way. "Let me die and get it over with," Jessie says in Didion's *Democracy*. "Let me be in the ground and go to sleep."[2]

That was the year, like Didion's twenty-eighth in "Goodbye to All That" but later, when I was discovering that "not all of the promises would be kept, that some things are in fact irrevocable and that it had counted after all, every evasion and every procrastination, every word, all of it."[3] I was living in Joshua Tree, on the edge of a national park, with someone who barely tolerated me but more than anyone else, and I could no longer tell myself I was not a writer because I did not have the time. I was not a writer because I no longer enjoyed my own thoughts. I could not write my way to calm. I looked out from a wall of picture windows onto 500,000 acres of protected wilderness, and the view never seemed to change. Instead I rearranged my collections, of pottery and rocks, every day for maybe hours, or I noticed things wrong, like a mustard-yellow corduroy couch in the midcentury style and made myself hysterical over its immense wrongness. Of course, in her four-room floor-through in New York Didion decorated through malaise, too, hanging yards of yellow silk across her bedroom windows, "because I had some idea that the gold light would make me feel better, but I did not bother to weight the curtains correctly and all that summer the long panels of transparent golden silk would blow out the windows and get tangled and drenched in afternoon thunderstorms."[4]

One day, I was complaining again on the phone to a friend about the mustard couch, which he had refused to get rid of, and she said, why don't *you* just get rid of it, and once in a while it is easier to take good advice. I could not get any of the donation centers in town to pick it up, not the one for victims of domestic abuse, not the one for survivors of suicide. I could not ask him to help me load it in my car, and so I was dragging it out the door when he came home. Where are you taking my couch, he asked. The thrift store, I said. They'll never accept such a ratty thing, he said of the couch, it has to go to the dump. He'd have his guys handle it. Then the couch was gone. Until years later when we were moving away, and I saw the couch again, hidden behind a trailer on the far side of the land, surrounded by beer cans and cigarette butts, where everyone but me would hang out.

My affliction was mostly the commonplace that my life was beautiful and small, that I was loved and no bombs fell around me, and in the presence of this luck I "meditated on my desolation,"[5] as John Lahr wrote of Didion, not in flattery. There was plenty of pioneering optimism in the desert, and after the market crash there were square acres of land for $10,000, but most days what I felt in the air was a certain dry inertia that comes from surviving too many days of worry that your life might be slipping away, and who knows why we ever do not do what it is we should have done. I did not do anything for an entire year that accumulated. I was as incapacitated and negligent as Didion purported to be. How long have I thought of melancholia as an accompaniment to her sentences, and malaise the buttress to her observations, as something not only glamorous and literary but necessary to seeing. She wrote "In Bed," an essay in *The White Album*, about spending "one or two days a week almost unconscious with pain"—a luxury afforded by forgiving editors, forgiving partners, forgiving bank accounts—a "shameful secret, evidence not merely of some chemical inferiority but of all my bad attitudes, unpleasant tempers, wrongthink."[6] But, of course, these migraines are not a secret anymore, and not particularly shameful, apparently. Didion is writing about it, and this suffering gifts her with subject matter, and then again:

> "The migraine has acted as a circuit breaker, and the fuses have emerged intact. There is a pleasant convalescent euphoria...I notice the particular nature of a flower in a glass on the stair landing. I count my blessings."[7]

It makes me want to have a migraine, which is not quite right. It makes me want a stair landing. Didion writes of lost days pushing cut orchids around in a bowl of water, and also later, in

The Year of Magical Thinking, about dying and being left behind, "the relentless succession of moments during which we will confront the experience of meaninglessness itself."[8] Her stand-ins find no reason to go on either, like, "I know something that he never knew. I know what 'nothing' means,"[9] says Maria, who from her mother "inherited my looks and a tendency to migraine,"[10] in *Play It As It Lays*. I mistook fatalism as the content of her writing when it was always the substrate, all that nothing holding up her words over and over. Her despondency is an outlook. I, too, tried to think of my depression as a critical sensibility, or why I found things interesting but not delightful, but sometimes the reason for malcontent is chemical, and sometimes it attaches to an arbitrary aesthetic fastidiousness, and sometimes it finds a real mark, but when there is a structural, external reason for the estrangement we call it grief or revolution, not depression.

The story goes that Gloria Steinem was getting in a car one day when someone asked her if she had any thoughts on Joan Didion, and Steinem said, "Ask her how come, if she spends all her time crying and swimming and struggling to open a car door, she finds the energy to write so much?" Steinem has described depression as anger turned inward, and as a lamentable malediction upon women, self-inflicted or otherwise. Anger, she insists, is invigorating and I imagine she's right about that, and action even better. Steinem might not have trusted the possible coexistence of doing and despair, but I have to. I suspect this is what makes Didion such a beacon, for so many writers or at least the emotionally unstable. I cried reading Steinem's memoir, *My Life on the Road*, or more specifically I cried reading the dedication page, where she recalls the doctor who performed her abortion extracting two promises: that she would never tell anyone his name, and that she would do what she wished with her life.

"Dear Dr. Sharpe, I believe you, who knew the law was unjust, would not mind if I say this so long after your death:

I've done the best I could with my life.

This book is for you."[11]

I am not like Steinem; I have not done the best I could with my life. I am not strong enough to deserve the shoulders of those who came before. But I would hope to be allowed an abortion anyway, if only to squander the time afterward. I am a mess, and even worse: I consider a certain starchy tidiness to be inelegant and belabored.

Didion claims that she does not appear fastidious to others, but rather like someone who gives herself a little license: "'You don't look like a migraine personality,' a doctor once said to me. 'Your hair's messy. But I suppose you're a compulsive housekeeper.' Actually my house is kept even more negligently than my hair, but the doctor was right nonetheless." How the doctor was right is the answer to Steinem's question. Didion is a perfectionist whose perfectionism takes "the form of spending most of a week writing and rewriting and not writing a single paragraph," which even Steinem would have to agree is preferable to housework.[12]

This seems also, perhaps, the gentlest, truest thing I might say of all the words I did not write in the desert. In those debilitated days when I did not write and was not a writer, when I only rearranged rocks, in those days when nothing interfered with my writing but the weakness of my character and the limitations of my talent, in those days when no one cared whether I got up or not—sometimes, yet, I did. Didion has been accused so often of glamorizing depression, but instead what she's glamorizing is the slim possibility of depression not hollowing one out, of despair and doing. I could still get out of bed today, and still move to

Mexico with him as we did, and still hope to write a poem he would love as much as I love his work, or at least I could finish this sentence. I can still try, through the sheer plain sadness, to do the best with my life.

ENDNOTES:

1. Joan Didion, "Some Dreamers of a Golden Dream," in *Slouching Towards Bethlehem* (New York: Farrar Straus and Giroux, 1968), 3.
2. Joan Didion, *Democracy* (New York: Simon & Schuster, 1984), 60.
3. Joan Didion, "Goodbye to All That," in *Slouching Towards Bethlehem* (New York: Farrar, Straus and Giroux, 1968), 233.
4. Didion, "Goodbye to All That," 232.
5. John Lahr, *Automatic Vaudeville* (New York: Alfred A. Knopf, 1984).
6. Joan Didion "In Bed," in *The White Album* (New York: Simon & Schuster, 1979), 167.
7. Joan Didion, "In Bed," 171.
8. Joan Didion, *The Year of Magical Thinking* (New York: Random House, 2007), 189
9. Joan Didion, *Play It as It Lays* (New York: Farrar, Straus and Giroux, 1970), 214.
10. Didion, *Play It as It Lays*, 5.
11. Gloria Steinem, Dedication, *My Life on the Road* (New York: Random House, 2015).
12. Joan Didion, "In Bed," 170.

The Opposite of Cool

By Joshua Wolf Shenk

IN THE FALL OF 2005, at the shuttle terminal of New York's LaGuardia airport, I entered the security line and noticed, in front of me, a slight, and slightly stooped, older woman. After a couple of blinks, I recognized Joan Didion.

I had just published my first book and was going to Boston— en route to Harvard Square—for the first stop of a small tour. Didion had just published *The Year of Magical Thinking.* I introduced myself and, with some diffidence, told her how much she had influenced me, and could I give her a copy of the book I had just published, my first?

Didion held a single, slight leather bag in her left hand. She looked at me with what seemed like a mild panic. "Can you send it to me?" she asked, with some diffidence of her own. I realized immediately what she meant, that the additional weight in her bag would be more weight than she could bear.

That afternoon, I gave my reading at the Harvard Bookshop in Harvard Square. When I finished, the store clerk who had kindly tended to me said she was now off to set up for Didion herself, at a Unitarian church down Massachusetts Avenue. She offered to save seats for me and two friends who had come to my reading.

That night, I watched from a pew as Didion, in an armchair, read a passage from *Magical Thinking*. After she finished, a long queue formed for the signing. I asked the bookstore clerk if she might take my copy of the book to Didion for her signature at the end of the rush. Several days later, the book arrived in the mail to my apartment in Brooklyn.

Of course, I recognized the signature. But no matter how many times I blinked, I could not make out the several words Didion had inscribed. It was a slight scrawl, delicate but inscrutable. I tried to resign myself to not understanding it. I put the book on my shelf, but now and again I couldn't help myself—I would pick it back up and try again.

◆◆◆

I SUPPOSE THAT I came to live in Los Angeles, in a roundabout way, because of the Bricklin. This was a car, made in 1974 and '75 in a volume of roughly three thousand units, by a serial automotive entrepreneur named Malcolm Bricklin. They were striking cars, low-slung, with electric gull-wing doors, and a fiberglass body covered by acrylic resin. But the company soon failed, in part because of a fatal flaw: the electric doors drew so much power that the battery would quickly drain and die.

My grandfather was a wholesaler. He bought big lots of odd products whose makers could not sell them. He bought the unsold Bricklins and sold them from his warehouse in Columbus, Ohio. One of these cars came to my dad.

I was four or five at the time, and the Bricklin became an emblem of my youth in Cincinnati. The color of a light brown M&M, it had a long snout like a Ferrari, and a big growl.

It smelled faintly of gas. It had a space behind the two bucket seats where two of us—we were three brothers—would clamber. I remember the snug rush of driving in the Bricklin while in the back. I remember, too, standing next to it in a parking lot, hearing the impotent click of the black plastic door switch as my dad jammed his finger against it—waiting, in vain, for the muscular hum of the door that was supposed to follow. The Bricklin was exotic and doomed.

My dad moved onto other fascinations with motion. He was always drawn to emotion-laden cars and, when he came into money in my teenage years, he studied for his pilot's license and began to fly small prop planes. When I was in middle school, I think, he stowed the Bricklin in a warehouse somewhere.

Then, nearly three decades later, he pulled it out. An eccentric, sentimental, and, by then, wealthy man, my dad had the Bricklin rebuilt by an engineer from the original factory. The door mechanisms were remade to open and close by force of air. The body was repainted yellow (just, as it happens, like Joan Didion's 1969 Corvette Stingray).

When my brother David saw the refurbished Bricklin, he said he wanted to throw up. He saw in it my dad's profligacy, and I understood. But I found the car dazzling. I felt a glow in my stomach thinking about it, and I let the feeling of that Bricklin, and my longing for that feeling, hover in the air above me.

◆◆◆

I LIVED MOST OF my young adult life in cities where people and buildings lean against each other like deep drunks in a bar. In the twenty years after I left college, I made a small life in letters, and I made good friends, and then I made a mess of a relationship with a woman I asked to marry me but never married. Three years into our warm but fraught intimacy, she became pregnant with our son, around the time that my father fell seriously ill.

In 2009, with my son growing in utero—and my father holding onto life only tenuously—I visited Los Angeles and became intoxicated by its lightness, and its cool, which I felt as keenly as I smelled the pungent spring blooms. I saw a number of old friends and it struck me incessantly how much less pressure came down on them than my people in New York. I felt scared and penned in at the time. I came to ascribe this feeling to the subways and galley kitchens, all those people in so little space. New York had come to feel like one of those pieces made by the artist Do Ho Suh, where thousands of plastic figures are pressing their hands up against a plate of glass.

On the way back east after that trip, I stopped to visit my dad in Colorado. My fiancée met me there and, in between long stretches sitting at his bedside, I had a vision. It came on me like a soft-focus film still, a vision of myself driving the Bricklin on an LA freeway. It was not a vision in the sense of an idea to guide meritorious actions. It was a vision in the sense of a primal image, a dark desire.

◆◆◆

IN FEBRUARY 2011, THE vision materialized in a surprising way because, just as my son's mom and I split up, she suddenly left her job and accepted an offer to work in public radio in Santa Monica. I came along, to follow her, to be near my thirteen-month-old son, and because of my vision. I had a book to write, so I felt portable. I told friends LA would be an "adventure."

My son's mom moved to a warm, modest neighborhood of bungalows, a few blocks east of Lincoln Boulevard. Her place had a converted garage, across a cozy garden sheltered by a high wall, that she used as the baby's room. Because she looked at prospective homes with presence and love, she always found good enclosures.

By contrast, I rented a one-room apartment near Venice Beach, which felt like a perch from which I would fly into a grand unknown. This chronic absence from my experience—the psychiatric diagnosis is dissociative disorder—often leaves me cold to myself and other people. In this furnished studio, I eyed the single bed with some foreboding. Either it would be a problem—because it had no room to share with someone—or I would have a problem, because I would have no one to share it with. (It turned out to be the latter.) The apartment had two substantial closets, one large enough to fit a crib of the Pack 'n Play variety. This seemed reasonable to me at the time, but when my friend Josh saw the makeshift crib in the closet he asked, "Should I be worried about you?"

I hoped I would find, in LA, space to unclench and light to color up my darkness. Yet, I found myself ill at ease, even though every day was sunny and in the seventies. I thought LA would be a softer way to live but I was surprised at its hard edges.

"The sunshine is *invasive*," my friend Lynne Tillman says of LA. It took me years to grasp the basic physics, that less moisture in the air means the light is refracted less, and thus felt more keenly or—the word that feels most right is *sharply*. When I go back to Cincinnati or farther east, what it feels like to me—at least spring to fall—is soft. And *lush*. This word is onomatopoeia. I feel its meanings as I say it, quietly, in my mouth. Growing luxuriantly. Providing great sensory pleasure.

It took me years to really see how my constitution was ill suited to a place as dry as Los Angeles. And as cool.

◆◆◆

I CAN'T REMEMBER WHAT happened to my Bricklin idea. I think my stepmother quashed it. I guess it was fitting that an *idea* of a car, and an *idea* of a city, would recede, in the actual light of actual LA, to the drab question of how I would get myself around. First I rented a car at a monthly rate, but I dithered so thoroughly on what to do for a permanent solution that I returned the expensive rental and went to a rent-a-wreck place on Lincoln Boulevard.

This car, a nineties American sedan, did not, I don't think, *actually* tilt slightly to the right. And it did not, I don't think, actually have one of those old ashtrays with a bottom coated by tar. I am, I think, making up these images to populate the actual feeling of this sad, beaten car and, with the car, the coming sense that my neuroticism and indecision and financial worries—I had a book contract, but the years it would take to deliver it stretched ahead of me—made me ill-suited for a life in the golden land.

I remember driving that wreck to a friend's house in Laurel Canyon, which had a gate, and a narrow passage up a steep hill, and a landing on top where she and her husband parked a baby blue Prius and a British Racing Green Land Rover. I admired my friend's style so much I found myself wishing I could walk around her house with my phone's QR reader, extracting the e-commerce sites where I might acquire each piece, but I knew the thing I really admired I could not acquire—which was their cool, the effortlessness with which her husband hacked off the stems of kale stalks over his kitchen sink, and with which my friend served strawberries in a modern bowl from an artisan's kiln. I later asked him where would he suggest I buy a good kitchen knife, but I never had the temerity to ask her where they got their pottery, for not asking, not noticing so much even, and certainly not imitating—this somehow seemed an essential part of the vibe.

Leaving their mid-century house and putting my son into a car seat in the back seat of the wreck felt like leaving the set of a life I wished I could play on.

◆◆◆

In those early months, I made U-turns. I made one on my way to meet a guy for dinner in Culver City, and I made one trying to get to an interview in the Pacific Palisades. I was constantly trying to read the lines on the small screen of my phone against the road—and to correlate the red pin on the map against a mass of undifferentiated parking lots in L-shaped strip malls. I did not do this well. It wasn't unusual for me to do three or four U-turns—turning around because I missed a place, missing it again, turning around...

The car I ended up buying, a used Nissan Altima hybrid, had a wide turning radius, so "U-Turn" often actually meant a three-point, and sometimes four-point, turn. I came to decide that when I someday got another car, a tight turning radius ought to be a priority.

◆◆◆

The spring following my brief encounter with Didion, I took my signed copy of *Magical Thinking* with me to a class I taught at the New School, where I had assigned the students to identify what I called a writer's "central preoccupation." I got this phrase from my teacher Pat Hoy, to name that vein of thought, or concern, that ran through all of an artist's work. If mined, Pat suggested, it can yield the pure ore of an artist's sensibility. And he thought this exercise in reading would improve writing, which proceeds from opening those same veins in ourselves.

After a long discussion with my class, what emerged, with Didion, was her preoccupation with place, with site, with a repetition—bordering on perseveration—of specific locales. In Didion, it's not the house but the house on Franklin Avenue and not Richard Carroll but Richard Carroll in Beverly Hills and not a hospital but the "Beth Israel Medical Center's Singer Division, at that time a hospital on East End Avenue (it closed in August 2004) more commonly known as 'Beth Israel North' or 'the old Doctor's Hospital.'"[1]

Of course, all writing depends on specificity. But my class agreed that, with Didion, this specificity felt psychologically critical—like a plant reaching its roots in thin soil in a bitter wind. Something about Didion seemed attenuated, alienated, and, yes, dislocated.

I loved this conversation. I loved how my students had found something hidden in plain sight—at once clear and beguiling. And, as the conversation peaked, I looked again—it had become a habit—at the title page of my book. And I swear, right then, the lines from Joan Didion's hand finally emerged from ether to words.

For Josh,
Joan Didion
From the shuttle!

◆◆◆

THEY SAY THAT LOS Angeles rivals Florida as the recovery capital of the world, and I spent a good portion of my early years there going to twelve-step meetings. I tried a variety of them. I wasn't sure whether food, or cannabis, or money was the main issue.

One day, I went to an Overeater's Anonymous meeting at a house in Beachwood Canyon, not far from the world headquarters for The Church of Scientology, and at the foot of the Hollywood Hills (a phrase always tinged for me with the song "Hollywood

Nights" by Bob Seger, whom my dad took me to see at Riverfront Coliseum in Cincinnati, who sang of the "Midwestern boy on his own").

The meeting was in an old, faded mansion off Franklin Avenue, and suddenly, after so many times reading Didion's essay "The White Album," I felt I had found a physical correlate to the twenty-eight-room house she describes there, in a neighborhood—as she says—where decrepit mansions were being rented monthly, and were, therefore, popular among therapy groups and rock bands.

Many people will say that Didion embodies LA, that she articulates its essential idea. The more I thought about it, the more I came to see that the two are as common as disparate air molecules in the same room. Joan Didion is LA—not because of anything she said about its geography, or its people, or history. It's the tone. It's the weightlessness. It's the cool.

Cool has been the subject of academic monographs and museum exhibitions, but it can't be analyzed, obviously, or even grasped. It's not a matter of any substance, but an erotic idea.

Erotic is what we desire that is out of reach, inducing greater desire. And because we humans are ill-suited to recognize that we are cats drawn endlessly to paw at strings that hang from on high, we tell stories about the erotic to try to domesticate it. The dumbest of those stories are pornography. The most glossy are on the cover of *Vanity Fair*. They are all gods that fail, of course, and we are caught in the thrum of the unreachable, from which we reach harder still.

Didion's reputation has caught this whorl, and ascended high. The irony is that this has led us to see her ineptly. Not long ago, I talked over dinner with an LA poet who meditates several hours a day and whose descriptions of her psychological state in these sessions made me think of the effect in *Star Trek* where a body moves from presence to ether. Anyway, this poet was going on and on about how courageous Didion is, about how much she *reveals*.

Of course, I recognized her data points. It is startling, indeed, to reprint portions of one's psychiatric record, as Didion did in "The White Album," or to write, in the famous line from Didion's first *LIFE* column, in 1969, "We are here on this island in the middle of the Pacific in lieu of filing for divorce."[2]

These are bold declarations indeed but they are not revelations, and they are certainly not confessions. A confession is when someone breaks down and tells you everything on a particular subject, and I don't know that Joan Didion has ever done that.

She does not collapse on the stage. She darts onto it, and says the most stunning thing, and then darts off. It is not the weight of her disclosures that stuns the audience, but the lightness of attention as it hovers between there and not there, between her enticing proximity and her blunt distance. Joan Didion is not a penitent in confession, or a lover ready for embrace. She is not even a burlesque dancer. God no. She is a boxer. She floats like a butterfly and stings like a bee.

◆◆◆

THERE IS NOW A considerable literature against Didion—"a standard critique of the legend,"[3] writes Constance Grady, in *Vox*. The critique is that she's a legend, indeed—a popular story that is unauthenticated.

The legend's moniker is "St. Joan." And Didion is an object of secular worship in modern letters. I recently talked with an editor at FSG who told me that an applicant for an assistant position was asked which writers he found overrated, and the editor was amused when the candidate answered Joan Didion. "I admire your temerity," he said to the applicant, "though I must question your taste."

To criticize her often seems, beyond poor taste, a kind of sacrilege, especially after *Magical Thinking*, which seem to embody the most profoundly human, vulnerable experience of grief.

It is too bad, though, that people misread *Magical Thinking*—that even the most discerning bookstores shelve it as memoir. It's not a memoir of grief. It is, quite explicitly, an essay about *alienation from grief*—or, I suppose you could say, the alienation often bound up in grief. But this alienation, in all forms, has long been Didion's true subject.

"As a writer," Didion writes in *Magical Thinking*, "even as a child, long before what I wrote began to be published, I developed a sense that meaning itself was resident in the rhythms of words and sentences and paragraphs, a technique for withholding whatever it was I thought or believed behind an increasingly impenetrable polish."[4]

We could call this polish "cool." Recall the exchange at the hospital where her husband was rushed to after his heart attack, when the social worker approaches with a doctor. Didion writes: "'He's dead, isn't he,' I heard myself say to the doctor. The doctor looked at the social worker. 'It's okay,' the social worker said. 'She's a pretty cool customer.'"[5]

On the page Didion is the epitome of control, mastery, and clarity. But this order seems to proceed from a chronic sense of meaninglessness, detachment, and distress. In *Blue Nights*—which came out in 2011, and which I read, avidly, in my early U-turn days in LA—Didion suggests that her alienation through writing has made for a kind of constrictor knot. For, the more she pulls at it with her writing, the tighter it gets, since her writing is the essential mechanism for her disassociation. Didion says she started *Blue Nights* thinking she would write about children, but she discovered the "actual subject was this refusal to even engage in such contemplation."[6] In the book, she flays herself for how she has gone missing from her own experience, but in that mesmerizing voice that has been the key for her escapes all along.

Didion does evince a *wish* to know her thoughts, for them to be, as she writes in *Magical Thinking*, finally "penetrable, even if only for myself."[7] And we can all empathize with this struggle. We are all, one way or another, on a fulcrum between meaning and meaningless, between blunt knowledge and narcotic abandonment. Yet, while energized by that fulcrum, Didion's work always ends up swinging one way. In an interview with KPFK in Los Angeles in 1972, Didion said her character Maria in *Play It as It Lays* "is coming to terms with the meaninglessness of experience." This is Didion's leitmotif. If I hadn't come to live in this city I would be less pained about what she said next. "And that's what everybody who lives in Los Angeles essentially has to come to terms with because none of it seems to mean anything."[8]

◆◆◆

WHAT HAD BEGUILED ME about Los Angeles was the prospect of finding a home. I stared with longing at the photographs of staged living rooms and, lured by these images, drove to Mar Vista, Laurel Canyon, Studio City, Silver Lake, and South Pasadena.

I guess I thought that the right physical space—the weight of being held on a plot, under beams, behind glass, within a walled garden—would open me into something I couldn't then, and can't still name, and which I ineptly allude to only when I call it that elusive cool.

Then, when I was living in a small two-bedroom apartment, near Pico and Lincoln—certainly one of the ugliest, if not *the* ugliest—intersections in America, my father died. It was not a surprise, because of his long illnesses, but it was still very much a shock. I was also shocked by my new financial reality. I had been looking at small bungalows and beaters and could now consider the sorts of architectural gems represented by major realtors.

And so I bought this stunning house, a block from the Silver Lake Reservoir, and I learned that living within the awed stillness of a masterpiece of residential architecture did nothing to alleviate my distinct mental alienation.

◆◆◆

IT WAS NOT UNTIL later that it occurred to me to think of the relationship between architectural photography and porn. You can get aroused looking at a photograph, and then imagine a relationship with the subject—or object—of the photograph. This does evoke an actual physiological feeling. And you can act on it. But it will then declare itself a fantasy. It's warmth like from an electric shock, as opposed to warmth from baseboard heat.

Consider the iconic image of the "Stahl House" in the Hollywood Hills. This photograph, taken by Julius Shulman, with the help of two assistants, in May 1960, is considered the most famous architectural photograph of all time, and is a central image to the iconography of modern LA.

One recent morning, I spent a long time looking at this photograph and reading about how it was made. The house arose in the first place out of a quest for good images. The Case Study houses, of which this was #22, were commissioned by *Arts & Architecture* magazine, which facilitated these experiments in modernism in exchange for exclusive photographs of the results.

The Stahl House took this imagism to an extreme. For, after Shulman's photograph became such a sensation, the Stahl family began to rent out their house for film shoots and commercial photographers—so much so that it became their sole income. An image made a reality, which was later claimed again by the image.

Faced with an image of this sort, a surface of "impenetrable polish," how does one enter?

In the Shulman image, the glass box of the house designed by the architect Pierre Koenig extends into the cavernous sky, beyond which lay the glow of the evening lights of Los Angeles. Shulman used a seven-minute exposure to make those lights pop, and he laid over it a second exposure he made to capture two women facing one another, as though at a cocktail party. At least, I used to read them as women at a party—amidst a bustling, elegant, and connected life inside this well-appointed, startling home.

The women in the photograph, it turns out, were extras recruited for the shoot. (One was dating the architect's assistant.) The house was unfinished, dusty with construction, the furniture staged for the shoot.

But these details of image making are less interesting than the declarations of the image itself. Like Didion, the inability to enter Shulman's photograph is its erotic core. It tells you, as she does, that you can't come in, and yet legions of us, like birds against glass, still keep trying. (Twice now, below the large glass windows in my own Silver Lake home, I have found dead birds, and twice my son and I have buried them in the sod at the side of the artificial turf in our backyard.)

Within Shulman's shot, there is no sight line that shows you how you might get in the house. The more I looked at it, the more the question arose in me: How *would* one get in? When I shared this image with my friend Erica, who is more empathetic than me, she said she always had the same feeling—but focused on the women in this image, that they are trapped in a glass box they cannot leave.

When I looked at the photograph, I looked and looked, because I could not, for the life of me, find an elegant way to describe the feeling. I felt the desire well up in me, and the longing, and the impotence, until I finally wrote something dumb and blunt and awkward. I wrote something not at all cool. "I want to fuck this photograph," I wrote.

◆◆◆

I HAD BEEN IN Los Angeles for three years or so when I heard something that felt like a revelation about why I could not fit in the place, why I felt so attenuated, why I could not get the thing that I wanted, which is another way of talking about how my shadow desire—my desire to keep myself in a shadow—is so copiously fed there.

What I heard was a small story told by a big writer and director for film and television. She was talking, casually, about a time she had gone to work on the writing staff for an award show—the Emmys, or the Grammys, or something like that. She went to write bits and sketches, and she brought an old colleague on with her, and she was embarrassed, she told me and some others at brunch in her casual, warm, stylish house in Silver Lake, when this colleague got upset on the set one day.

The trouble was not that my friend's colleague was upset, but that she *showed* she was upset. My friend was horrified, she said, though she recounted this emotion over brunch with a calm so thorough that I, myself, would need to be medicated to replicate it. "Everyone knows," she said in a voice as close to affectless as I have known, "that the only person on a set who is allowed to have emotions is the star."

I remember a plastic tray with fruit and lox and bagels. I remember a drum set in the living room. I remember being struck that I had just received the tiny silver key that would turn the mechanism in the intricate silver lock that would explain my experience of Los Angeles.

◆◆◆

NOT LONG AFTER THAT, I rented my own home for a commercial shoot. It was good money. Midday, I came to the house to fetch something I needed, and, as I was ready to leave, the next scene or shot commenced, and we all needed to be quiet, and still.

So I stood around and watched. I wasn't interested in the action and I have no memory of it. I was interested in the guy with the belly next to the light on a black plastic pole, and the woman with the Starbucks cup slouching with a clipboard. I was interested in what it would be like to stand around like that all day. To be still, and inconspicuous, while an image is made for the screen.

◆◆◆

AFTER FOUR YEARS IN LA, I did something that seems so absurd, given my struggle with the brightness of the sunshine, and the dryness of the air, and the loneliness of driving so much. I picked up and took a job in Las Vegas.

The applicable cliché, of course, is *out of the frying pan into the fire*. I moved from a semi-arid climate to a properly austere desert. In Las Vegas I keep two humidifiers running in my one-bedroom apartment, and I fill those vessels fastidiously. (I am not a desert amphibian, I have come to reckon. I am a swamp frog.)

But while Las Vegas in many ways represents Los Angeles taken to its absurd extremes, it is also its perfect inverse. LA, for all its immigration, is still an exclusive city. The iconic architectural detail in LA is the gate, or the thick hedge, or the wall separating dominant local institution—film studios—from people who are not on the list. The rest of the city is built like a film set—long, ugly stretches that resolve in spectacular spaces that, typically, are quite private. "We don't go for strangers in Hollywood,"[9] says a character in Fitzgerald's *The Last Tycoon*.

Las Vegas, by contrast, is all strangers. Sometimes it feels like Ellis Island in the Mojave. In one of the casinos, the workers wear name tags that identify their hometown. The place you're from gives you identity here, and with that freshness comes a sense of the future as something that will be collectively made.

Climate aside, Las Vegas is obviously the opposite of cool. David Foster Wallace called it "the least pretentious city in America."[10] In his foundational essay about the city, "At Home in the Neon," Dave Hickey celebrates even its venality as a virtue, for "what is hidden elsewhere," he writes, "exists here in quotidian visibility."[11] In Las Vegas, access is flattened; the suppression of social differences, not their heightening, is the common drive; the iconic image is not the wall, but the neon sign. All in all, the city itself—not the Strip, which is to life for Las Vegans what Times Square is to life for New Yorkers—is the most earnest place I have ever long laid my head.

But this is not goodbye to all that. While I spend large portions of time in Las Vegas, my son still lives in LA. (His mom settled in Burbank, in another warm enclosure.) And my life with him means a sort of ongoing half-life with the city. I own my dream home still, and I drive in Friday afternoons to fetch my son from school for a weekend of his playdates. (He is playing hide-and-seek right now with his nanny, who has come over to give me time to write the final lines of this essay.)

I would say that moving between Vegas and LA has induced a dislocation, but clearly it's made an old dislocation more salient. Perhaps that was what my shadow wanted all along.

My life in my house now runs over this schism, too. I rent it out on Airbnb so often, and I mind this business assiduously, that as much as it is lovingly tended to—there is, for instance, a whole wall of magnetic paint on which hover my son's third-grade class portrait and the prom picture of me with the first woman I loved—it is also a kind of set. Airbnb has sent professional photographers twice.

One time, not long ago, I had renters due at about 6:00 p.m. or so and a late-night flight. I went to dinner at a neighborhood place, and then I drove back to my street, because I was going to leave my car in front of the house and take a Lyft to LAX. So I decided to sit and work in my car for a half hour. It was fine, it was comfortable, I tilted the seat back. Also, from behind the hedge in front of the house, I could not see in, nor could they see me. But as the Lyft came about 7:30 p.m., I got my suitcase in the trunk, and I rolled it to the car, past a sight line on the small driveway. There I caught a glimpse into the house. From the darkness on the street, I saw my foyer and, standing there, the folks I had rented the house to—a stylish couple from Seoul, in town for a fashion show.

The foyer. The place I'd often laced my son's shoes. The place I'd taken coats from friends. The place I hung tote bags and baseball hats. Through the glass next to the front door, I could clearly see these unfamiliar and elegant people standing there. It was as if this primal space in my life had become the set for one of their scenes, and I certainly could not enter.

ENDNOTES:

1. Joan Didion, *The Year of Magical Thinking* (New York: Alfred A. Knopf, 2005), 7.

2. Joan Didion, "A Problem of Making Connections", *LIFE*, December 5, 1969, 34.

3. Constance Grady, *Vox*, "What Joan Didion's new book, *South and West*, explains about her sensibility," April 7, 2017. https://www.vox.com/culture/2017/4/7/15161314/joan-didions-south-west-review

4. Didion, *The Year of Magical Thinking*, 7.

5. Didion, *The Year of Magical Thinking*, 15.

6. Joan Didion, *Blue Nights*, (New York: Alfred A. Knopf, 2011), 54.

7. Didion, *The Year of Magical Thinking*, 8.

8. Sally Davis, *The Female Angst/Anais Nin, Joan Didion and Dory Previn*, KPFK radio interview, February 10, 1972. https://www.pacificaradioarchives.org/recording/bc0611

9. F. Scott Fitzgerald, *The Last Tycoon* (New York: Charles Scribner's Sons, 1941), 11.

10. David Foster Wallace, "Big Red Son," in *Consider the Lobster* (New York: Little, Brown and Company, 2006).

11. Dave Hickey, "At Home in the Neon," in *Air Guitar*, (Los Angeles: Art Issues Press, 1997), 23.

A Woman Apart

By Lauren Sandler

FOR A LONG TIME, I wanted Joan Didion's heart. I wanted her heart because of how I venerated the exacting lucidity and fearsome organization of her mind. I wanted her heart to be as messy as mine, but I could never find that mess etched on her pages. I couldn't see myself in her willowy limbs, or her biography, but perhaps inside her I could discover that we shared some primordial swamp of longing and shame and rage.

But even when her life became redefined by grief, even in her self-revelation, she remained unreachable. She may have shattered, but the glass between us didn't. Her later memoirs of enduring the deaths of her husband and daughter refused to offer the emotional enmeshment and catharsis I sought, even when she exposed, in writing, her survival of the unimaginable.

It's a lousy thing to gripe about. I'm not complaining that she didn't suffer enough, only noting the sheer control with which she carved her story of a life utterly out of control. That's what she makes; that's how she's made. Decades before those deaths, in an essay that she wrote in 1969 after a breakdown—her psychic rupture and the culture's alike—she tells us that she wants us to know, as we read her, precisely who she is and where she is and what is on her mind. She says she is someone who needs "to try harder to make things matter"[1]; perhaps the baby, for example, never the work. What matters is what she witnesses, not how she feels about it. And that's only a problem if you're her husband, or her daughter—or a reader—trying to connect with her feeling. It's become our Didion aphorism, that she writes to find out what she thinks—what she sees and what it means, as she writes. In the American chaos, she sees with startling clarity. That is where the meaning lies. It's not a place of passion.

Yet what once maddened me, I've come to embrace, and see today as powerfully antithetical to the once-and-future popular modes of writing and womanhood alike. For Didion, emotion is not currency, nor does it hold necessary or defining meaning. Nor will she exist as the mirror of any of us, and certainly not all of us. Such tenets and practices are at odds with what we expect of our women writers, our women at all. Didion's work remains, in a scriptural sense, in the world but not of it. There is no fray that claims her, no quicksand that she wades into alongside us, to be swallowed whole. "You are getting a woman who for some time now has felt radically separated from most of the ideas that seem to interest other people,"[2] she writes.

In "The Women's Movement," her thoughts on feminism's tidal Second Wave, Didion briefly admits to living in the shared womanhood she defines as "that dark involvement with blood and birth and death."[3] But her entry into the female fracas was not written to express solidarity but profound irritation—essentially, that the making of an omelet does not amount to indentured servitude. To note, there's a grand class issue in much of her writing, sometimes effective, sometimes galling. But that's a discussion for another essay. Didion would not become anyone's idea of a woman: the helpmate or the revolutionary. She would not politicize her gender. While the writing about death—so much messy death, yet written with absolute control—would come later in considering her own loss; the writing about blood and birth never would.

To that point, I often think of how Didion became a mother. Giving birth does not make a woman a mother, any more than motherhood makes one a woman. But consider how radically separate she lives from so many of us. On a New Year's sail off Catalina with a friend who'd starred opposite Ronald Reagan in *Bedtime for Bonzo,* talk was of cocktails and babies. After quite a few of the former, the friend suggested Didion contact a certain pediatrician to discuss adopting one of the latter. This pediatrician had patient files labelled Garbo, Garland, and Taylor, and was with Bobby and Jackie in the intensive care unit the night Kennedy was assassinated. Some time later the phone rang. A baby had been born. They drove to see friends in Beverly Hills, and got smashed there on drinks chilled with ice from a crystal bucket. Over the next few days, Didion tells us, she bought a layette at Saks and brought her daughter home in a silk-lined cashmere blanket. Then she bought a collection of pastel dresses and a parasol and planned a trip to Saigon. She wanted to report on the war. It didn't occur to her, she has written, that she shouldn't just bring the baby.

Didion deems the Saks layette worthy of storytelling—but not the miscarriages her biographer, and others, have written she suffered. Does she owe us that blood? The mess of her life back then, as she shares it, is when Roman Polanski spills red wine on the short silk dress she was buying at the moment Bobby Kennedy was shot—the dress she wore with dark glasses to her own wedding. She will not take off those glasses if she chooses not to. The self remains largely unexcavated, the mess largely unplumbed, compared to many of our brilliant female minds, even among those like McCarthy and Hardwick, whose rise came a decade earlier, built on pages of sex, yearning, doubt, loneliness. Such revelations are not Didion's fare. She fits neatly nowhere, not in the decades of women writers to follow, who have written in menses' ink, who have mined miscarriages and miscalculations, constructing connection through the medium of mess itself. She isn't interested in reflecting our personal chaoses, any more than she is interested in reflecting society. Alongside her exactitude in reporting and writing alike, this is where her power lies.

She has become a literal icon, an image of a holy figure, in part because she exists at a remote distance from the lives of her readers. Her iconography is the cigarette and the Stingray, and later, the Celine ads, not the work at all. But the work is what matters. She is the work and the work is her. This is what is evident in her writing about motherhood, marriage, the mania of an era, which swallowed so much of her generation. Yet she gazes, cigarette in hand, from the cathedral walls flanked almost entirely by a markedly different pantheon of female writer. To see only aspirational cool is to worship the icon, not the writing itself, to miss how she trains her eyes on the Babel, not Bethlehem, of her homeland and her era, the "odd things going around town."[4] On death, always death, finding its threat, its completion, everywhere, long before it so dramatically and wholly ransacked her own home. And how she enforces order in the anarchy, through absolute restraint, word after word, sentence after sentence. In detached observation she makes incomparable meaning from the meaningless. Meaning is not synonymous with opinion. That fact undergirds most of her writing. And yet, in our era of hot takes—

boiled in emotional hemorrhage—that distinction strikes me as utterly lost.

Didion gave *Slouching Toward Bethlehem* its name not just because the center famously could not hold, but for the entirety of the Yeats epigraph she chose: two long stanzas she said had vibrated in her head for years. *The best lack all conviction, while the worst/Are full of passionate intensity.*[5] During those years, she was an exception within a new vanguard of nonfiction, a New Journalism that exulted in mess, and the pugilism of nonstop opinion, guillotining so-called objectivity. Just as she opted out of the conventions of how a woman should write, or raise a child, she defined herself as separate from the journalists who brought the first person roaring into reporting, pasting together *what I see* with *what I think*. Manhattan was the headquarters of New Journalism's swaggering, tumescent male domain. Goodbye to all that, etc. Instead of pontificating on Dick Cavett, Didion excused herself to hang her curtains in the land of the golden dream, making meaning of America by cutting crystal of its senselessness.

Opinion has become the mess of our time, just as anarchic collapse defined Didion's 1960s. The blood that connects us today, regardless of identity, is one defined by the passionate intensity that troubled her in the years even before the Manson murders, before the Panthers, before Bobby Kennedy got shot. That blood does not bathe her in passionate intensity. That absence of passionate intensity may have frustrated me once, a younger me, who yearned to connect and see myself in her. That may have frustrated me when we were merely swirling in this political and cultural gyre, before we'd dropped fully into its depths. Now that we have, the only yearning I feel is for her clarity.

ENDNOTES:

1. Joan Didion, "In The Islands," in *The White Album* (New York: Simon & Schuster, 1979), 136.

2. Didion, "In The Islands," 134.

3. Joan Didion, "The Women's Movement," in *The White Album* (New York: Simon & Schuster, 1979), 117.

4. Joan Didion, "The White Album," in *The White Album* (New York: Simon & Schuster, 1979), 41.

5. William Butler Yeats, "The Second Coming," *Collected Poems* (New York: The MacMillan Company, 1924).

Where I Am From

By Michelle Chihara

JOAN DIDION GAVE THE valedictorian speech at her eighth-grade graduation. From the beginning, she seems to have always commanded the speaker's position. In a society that has a habit of responding as if women who speak publicly are hysterical or mad, in a society that often systematically excludes women from public life, Didion has always seemed a step ahead, somehow stronger than anyone who might deny her the podium. Of course, she enrages many. She was a skeptic of the feminist movement, a movement that probably opened some of the doors she stepped through. And yet for generations of women, for women with a range of reactions to the word "feminist," Joan Didion has set the stage. Her enemies might call her neurotic or elitist. No matter. She has already described her own neuroses and headaches, and done it with such insight and grace and detached cool that the charges never stick. In 2003, she published *Where I Was From*, a kind of semi-memoir written after her mother's death. It's a meditation on California and her family's relationship to the land, in which she turned the force of her insight on her own eighth-grade speech and its topic, "Our California Heritage."

As an eighth grader, Didion lionized the pioneers, her direct ancestors who came across the country in covered wagons. At the Arden School in Sacramento, she wore a pale green organdy dress and her mother's crystal necklace, marks of her inheritance. Then in 2003, she wrote to disavow this heritage. She wanted to process her grief as well as to slice through her mother's Old California pretenses. Didion wrote that embedded in her family's attachment to their past, to land in California, and to frontier heroism, there lay confusions about America. Note the past tense in the title *Where I Was From*. This is Didion's attempt to see her mother, her past, and the American Dream clearly. She wrote it to leave some aspect of her inheritance behind. In the book, somewhat heartbreakingly given what happened a few years later, Didion said she wanted to free Quintana Roo from her ghosts. She wrote that Quintana didn't need to grow up under the shadows of the Donner Pass. She didn't have to preserve old things just because they were old and belonged to the Didions.

And yet, the book feels haunted. Didion can, as she puts it, only approach these topics "obliquely."[1] On the one hand, she clearly hopes to disable any sense of entitlement. Just because the Didions can trace their bloodlines back eight Californian generations, Quintana is not landed gentry. Didion was raised to think of herself as almost frontier nobility and she wants to puncture that myth. On the other hand, she writes Old California too well. She conjures the mystique she says she wants to dispel. I still find myself circling around *Where I Was From*, its beautiful and oblique writing. I often revisit it, a long exercise in Didion's singular ability to aestheticize cognitive dissonance. She looks at hard truths directly, unflinchingly. But then she lends Old Sacramento and the frontier mythos her trademark style.

Didion tells you that the crystal necklace will not protect you, but it glows on the page. She tells you that growing water-heavy crops in dry California is unsustainable and foolish. Then she paints the organdy dress in the pale green of new rice on the first days of spring. Being told something is foolish does not inoculate a reader against a longing for pale green organdy dresses. Didion wrote that because Quintana Roo was adopted, the ghosts on the old wooden Sacramento boardwalk did not belong to her. Joan was all that need matter to Quintana. Can you imagine being Quintana Roo? Can you imagine being told that all of the Didion myths and traditions, the fever dreams that haunted your commanding mother, were not yours? Not your inheritance? Wouldn't you still long for your mother's amulets and organdy dresses? Dear reader, I long for them still.

Didion almost always circled around her central topic. In this case, her central topic, her heritage, included a great deal of land in California. The central topic, the eighth-grade speech, and the book raise but then sidestep questions about Didion's role in the development of land. She unquestionably had an effect on the place she came from—which she sold, when her mother died and she left California mostly behind for New York. What about California belonged to her? What part of her belonged to California? She didn't come down on many concrete answers in *Where I Was From*. So in 2012, I tried to come up with some answers for her.

I wrote a chapter of a long and impossible dissertation about *Where I Was From* when I was a graduate student getting my PhD in contemporary American literature. I was also pregnant with my second daughter. After having spent seven years as a reporter and editor and freelance writer, I had gone back to graduate school and gotten married. In 2012, heavy with my second child, I was also heavy with the paralysis that motherhood brings. We couldn't afford for me to stay at home with the children, but I wasn't sure that we could afford any of my ambitions, either. I felt deeply ambivalent about where I was from and where I was going. I grew up in California, in Berkeley, eighty miles from Sacramento. I can't trace my family lines much beyond the Jewish pogroms and Japanese internments before and during World War II. I did not inherit land. My family's ghosts, of diaspora and displacement, were of the colonized variety. I'm the granddaughter of immigrants with my own desire to inhabit and puncture American myths. In the place of a long line of settled traditions, I had a library full of books. I wanted badly to find, in those books, answers on how to dispel ghosts and claim a space for my daughter. It's possible that I wanted to figure out, once and for all, how much of Didion's ability to command the stage was related to her heritage. In any case, I decided to look at her central topic more directly than she could. It seemed important to me, at the time, to pin down exactly how much of California belonged to Joan Didion.

The University of California awarded me a couple hundred dollars for a research trip. I flew to Sacramento from Los Angeles and dug into the state archives. I spent two days going through the public records, one by one, looking for the Didion family's land holdings. Was I doing academic or journalistic work? I'm not sure I can say. But I dug through hundreds of old records and maps, trying to track the sales of parcels that moved through multiple landholding partnerships. Some of these Didion names were in her book, some I tracked through her brother, James J. Didion. He had power of attorney for her mother when she died. I took many pictures of many documents.

More than six months pregnant, I was already waddling through pain in my hips. Sitting in a cubicle in the city assessor's office, I got the call from Kaiser with the results of my amniocentesis—the baby was healthy, and I was having a second daughter. I would be the mother of two daughters. I remember picking at state-issued Formica with my fingernail and murmuring quietly that yes, I could hear the nurse on the other end of the line. I would have to slice through the paralysis and puncture the myths for not one but two girls. For us all. I remember the beige of the particleboard desk, and not wanting to disturb other patrons of the assessor's office. I remember imagining that Didion would have approved of me in that moment. I didn't have a typewriter in my suitcase. My shapeless maternity dress was made of the kind of synthetic fabric that seems not to exist in her world. But I stayed cool and detached. Like her, I took the call and got back to work.

My findings, then…

In *Where I Was From*, Didion replaces a discussion of her own and her family's participation in the development of Californian land with a stylized and somewhat backhanded discussion of other land heiresses. She mentions the subdivision of land in the passive voice, as if it's an inevitable natural step into adult life: Didion's family moves into a house "on some acreage outside Sacramento until the time seemed right to subdivide the property."[2] Later, she mentions that she and her brother applied for a zoning change on a ranch they owned east of Sacramento, changing it from agricultural to residential. "New people" resist the Didions' zoning change. In her book, she segues from any discussion of her agency, as she and her brother went ahead and subdivided the ranch, to an account of aestheticized loss. She writes that her memory of Gilroy, where she and her father ate short ribs at the Milias Hotel among the potted ferns and dark shutters, is a hologram that dematerializes as she drives through it. The aesthetic disintegration of her memories is haunting, lovely. Perhaps inevitable. But the Didions chose to develop the land, over the protests of others. The zoning didn't vanish. How and when to develop was a decision the Didions made. The entire memoir sits as a book-length effort to look at and then mystify the Didion family's structural intervention in the California real estate markets.

Didion's brother, James J. Didion, is a powerful real estate tycoon. He had power of attorney for their mother, Eduene Didion, and was trustee of the Frank R. Didion family trust in the 1980s. It's his name that appears on most of the Didion family's land deals.

While her own name rarely shows up on the land records, Joan Didion states in the memoir that she and James made decisions about land together. On a 1998 title to a 48,352-square-foot plot of land (just over one acre) at Madison and Date Avenues in Sacramento, Joan signed as a counterparty for JJD Properties, one of a number of trusts and companies that appear under her brother's name. In the 1980s and 1990s, about eight acres of land in over ten discrete plots, transferred out of either that trust or from a member of Didion's immediate family, at Madison and Date alone.

The eight acres at Madison and Date make up less than half of the twenty-three or so acres that Didion family trusts developed in the decades before *Where I Was From*'s publication. Two streets, within this subdivided area, bear the name Jerrett, Didion's grandmother's name, and the name Didion. Those twenty-odd acres, in turn, represent a small fraction of the larger family's holdings. Didion writes in *Where I Was From* that the

Elizabeth Reese Estate Company, a corporation made up of her family as shareholders, owned a 640-acre ranch in Florin into her "adult life."[3] I found a mineral rights lease on 183 acres of Elizabeth Reese Company land that voided out in the 1970s. The twenty-three acres at Madison and Date alone must represent only one small group of sales.

I visited Didion Court, part of the Madison and Date development, in 2012. It was a cul-de-sac of single-story stucco houses with garages and small lawns that went up to the curb with no sidewalk—modest, stylistically unremarkable, subdivided plots. A temporary basketball net stood in a driveway. This was not the harsh and desolate inland empire of "Some Dreamers of the Golden Dream," it was the slack suburban postwar reality that Didion recognized made California rich. I tabulated the sales for the Madison Manor development nearby, which was developed before the 2008 financial crash by the Didions and Stamas Engineering. The sum total of all sales must have been significant.

In 2003, Didion wrote about land in Sacramento "where the vineyards got torn up so the Walmarts and the Burger Kings and the Taco Bells could grow."[4] Note the passive voice. Didion writes as if Walmart and the strip malls were a force of nature. She writes, in her paratactic rhythms, as if Taco Bells grow in a process unrelated to one group's ability to keep big box stores inland, away from residential properties at the coast. Another plot near Madison Manor that the Didions sold in 1985 held a strip mall and a car dealership when I saw it. The Didions granted an easement to the city for Highway 80 to cut through their land in 1972. A plot of land east of Highway 80, at Sunrise Boulevard and Old Auburn Road, has property records linking it to the Didion family as far back as 1850. In 1985 the Didions sold it to McDonald's.

Land use decisions are not a force of nature in a democracy. Development is a complicated process, but it's not a natural process. It's a political one. Didion writes about Native Americans coming into her great-great-great grandmother's house, as if the Native Americans too were a feature of the landscape. They were not. They were people with claims to the land. New people, white settlers in covered wagons, refused to recognize the native people's claims through a violent, unnatural series of wars. Power relations among new people and existing owners evolve, but always as politics. Activists and unions in Los Angeles once fought off a Walmart successfully. It is not biological evolution if Walmarts grow when planted. It's the struggle of history. Joan Didion left California, sold to McDonald's, and chose to re-zone the ranch. Her brother, whom she worked with to do this, was a powerful lobbyist for the National Realty Committee during the time when such lobbyists pushed to deregulate mortgage underwriting. He participated in the lead-up to the crisis in mortgage-backed securities in 2008. Powerful land-owning families play a role in how we build our cities, how we claim and imagine the land. I wanted Didion to cop to her role in the process.

Instead of discussing her own, or her brother's, ideas about developing land, Didion wrote about Jane Hollister Wheelwright and Joan Irvine, other land heiresses. She mocked Hollister Wheelwright for objecting to Chevron pipelines on her family's land, as if objecting to a pipeline could be nothing more than pernicious nostalgia. Meanwhile, the Didions held lease agreements with Shell Oil in the 1970s and Texas Oil & Gas in the 1980s, for mineral, oil, and gas rights on hundreds of acres of land in Sacramento. Instead of addressing her own family's pipelines, Didion wrote about Hollister's naivete in resisting a pipeline. She did not look at her brother's push for deregulation in the mortgage industry, as it might relate to her family's choices. She wrote about swallowing meat and telling her brother's children about cannibalism at the Donner Pass. She wrote a memoir, obliquely, about her idealized past in a Californian landscape where the vineyards *somehow got torn up*. In the passive voice. For Didion, the fast food franchises pop up with an "artless horror."[5] She swallows her own ability to look at her family's decisions. She looks away, and Californian dirt seems to come up in her mouth as the gothic return of the repressed.

◆◆◆

I HAVE BEEN CIRCLING around these thoughts since 2014. I wanted Didion to come clean, and yet in 2016, it got harder to keep my faith in the collective democratic processes that might have benefitted from her being more direct and honest. Didion wrote *Where I Was From* out of a gimlet-eyed urge to disengage, to cut loose from America's crazy myths. She felt bad about the Taco Bells and McDonald's. But she also mistrusted her own feelings, her desire to preserve things as they were, and she saw the need to let developers build for all the new people. Who can blame her for this? Now, in California with two daughters, I find I need her more than ever. In 1961, a young Joan Didion wrote for *Vogue* with a certain Victorian severity about the need for toughness, for moral nerve, in her essay, "On Self-Respect." Her metaphors back then were the colonizer's: she cited as a role model, of all people, the British general "Chinese" Gordon, with his stiff upper lip and self-sacrifice. People like him had self-respect, she wrote; they knew to give formal dinners in the rainforest. For them, "the candlelight flickering on the liana call forth deeper, stronger disciplines, values instilled long before. It is a kind of ritual, helping us to remember who and what we are."[6] In 2003, in *Where*

I Was From, Didion tried to move away from that Victorian severity. She tried to relinquish her mother's conservative faith in rituals and traditions. She tried to reimagine the organdy dresses and crystal necklaces as useless totems from a bygone world. Like formal dinners in the rainforest, they were nothing Quintana had to worry about. And yet she found nothing to replace them.

Didion skewered one-percenters like Joan Irvine and Jane Hollister Wheelwright; she shone a light on their pretenses. Perhaps it is her brother, James J. Didion, whom Joan failed to bring into focus. Immune as she was to some threats, she always leaned toward puncturing the myths of women. She was always hardest on herself first. She wanted to question her own impulse to protect the Milias Hotel. She knew that upper-class affectations can make you feel safe without keeping you safe, that the unblemished land would not barricade her against her own deeper "apprehension of meaninglessness."[7] She knew in 2003 that the levee wasn't holding.

In the end, all of my digging amounted to little more than my own swallowed effort to say to Joan Didion: Please don't give up on California. Keep the land, and the organdy dress, and wear it to dinner in the Mojave. Didion was trying to tell me, like she was trying to tell Quintana, that whatever haunts the wooden sidewalks in Sacramento was none of my business. And so I went there and walked those sidewalks, with my unborn daughter. I wanted to call her out, but in the end, I only did it because I wanted to walk beside her. Whether or not Joan Didion is now or has ever been rich, whether she is a good feminist or a good mother, a bad real estate developer or a good leftist critic—to quote Didion quoting her mother, *what difference does it make?* She belongs to California, and no one in journalism or academia has given me a better language than hers. I wish she hadn't mentioned Chinese Gordon. I wish she had gone easier on 1970s feminists. But she was right in other ways: We need rituals to help us remember who and what we are. I will not deed my Japanese Jewish Welsh American girls growing up in Los Angeles any acreage to speak of. So what do I have to offer them? Crystal necklaces. The collected works of Joan Didion. The names of California wildflowers. A promise to stay with our shared ghosts.

ENDNOTES:

1. Joan Didion, *Where I Was From* (New York: Vintage International, 2003), 15.
2. Didion, *Where I Was From,* 168.
3. Didion, *Where I Was From,* 12.
4. Didion, *Where I Was From,* 179.
5. Didion, *Where I Was From,* 73.
6. Joan Didion, "On Self-Respect," *Slouching Towards Bethlehem* (New York: Farrar, Straus & Giroux, 1968), 147.
7. Didion, *Where I Was From,* 205.

On Tour with a Reluctant Oracle

By Sarah Tomlinson

LIKE ANY NEW MOTHER, I was ecstatic and terrified. It was early 2015, and my first book, *Good Girl*, a daddy issues/coming-of-age memoir, was about to drop. As my day job, I'd ghostwritten ten memoirs—some huge *New York Times* bestsellers, some that had disappeared, like phantoms, with nary a trace. All the while, twenty-one years in total, I'd been on the bench, aspiring to publish a novel, and I had three completed in a drawer. *Good Girl* was something else entirely, but it would have its day.

As I prepared for the summit of my long-held publication fantasy—book tour—an instructive piece from Joan Didion's *The White Album* rose up: "On the Road." This is the essay (originally published in the August, 1977 issue of *Esquire* as "O My America") in which she lulls the reader into the hypnotic, deadening trance of shuttling through multiple cities at maximum velocity, seven appearances in a day. And instructs readers, via her shifting packing list: Her ideal of catching up on unanswered mail is abandoned partway through tour, to make room for her publisher's press releases, and "a thousand-watt hair blower."[1] All while chewing on the impossibility of answering the question being put to her: "Where are we heading?"[2]

As my in-house publicist, and the indie PR person I'd hired, scrambled to book me even one appearance in a day, I thought a lot about this piece, as an indication of how far we'd traveled as a culture. The type of book tour Didion had grudgingly endured in 1977 no longer existed in 2015. Our social media fever dream didn't allow for the same culture-wide interest in more than a few gilded writers, anointed each season. There weren't the same number of venues for publicizing books. With the exception of the celebrities for whom I ghosted, most writers didn't get invited to do talk shows anymore; they weren't celebrities in their own rights, as they once had been. Most people talked about how they needed to read more, rather than about what they'd recently read, if they talked about books at all. The career and life I'd dreamt of for two decades didn't exist anymore. I was going to have to deal with getting as far as I could on the fumes that were left. Only, I found I wasn't prepared to let go. Against the kind but firm advice of my literary agent, I spent my own money to replicate the type of multicity tour Joan had balked at, under the stress of wanting so badly to prove I had made it, to have the chance to weigh in on where we were heading.

My generous publisher gave me a bit of increasingly rare tour support. This, plus the money I earned as a ghostwriter, meant that I could afford to travel to nine events in eight cities over two months, where I talked to whoever would listen (including friends and family members who lived in/near those ports of call, and didn't need to read my book to know my story). It didn't look like the epic, crammed-to-the-quarter-hour itinerary Joan had withstood, but I persevered.

I wanted to be like Joan—anointed by culture, while at least appearing to have enough perspective to be detached from its notice, but the truth is I wasn't really listening to her. I was too busy trying to prove I was a writer with something to say, to heed the cautionary tale in that essay: "I was not sure what I was doing or why I was doing it,"[3] she wrote of what was also her first book tour, although she was publicizing her fourth book. This was my first book, but the ghostwriting made it feel like my nth. I craved the validation that telling my own story, and touring to promote it, would give me. Never mind Didion's clear warning that it probably wouldn't. And her clear advice about hair care. As photos of how disheveled I was looking by some of my latter events attest, I should have made room in my own luggage for a good hair blower.

On the surface of "On the Road," Joan is writing a send-up of the (sur)reality of book tour, rebelling against being tossed around the country, asked for her opinion again and again, only to feel that no one was listening, metaphorically. I found that no one was listening, literally. I couldn't convince the newspaper where I had freelanced for a decade to cover my book. None of the bookstores in my old home city would give me a reading. I hosted my own small book launch there, ending the night tipsy and despondent, the prodigal daughter who'd excelled, but not enough to be feted, or maybe just in the wrong arena. This was also my dad's hometown. We'd agreed he wouldn't come to my event because he just wasn't the kind of person who could do the normal dad stuff. And so, even though I'd healed our relationship through the writing of our story, I hadn't been able to make him into someone he wasn't. My first stop on the road.

It got harder.

My boyfriend had to coax me out of our hotel room before my Brooklyn bookstore event. Stress had caused me to break out.

I feared standing up in front of my agent, my publicists, and my friends and fellow writers and making a brash show of authority. Especially when I knew that, a month in, my book was not selling. And since it was not being reviewed much, and none of the dozen essays I had published online to promote it were going viral, it would not be selling.

In her writing, Joan pulled back her own artifice enough—literally let us peek in her suitcase at the "two 'good' suits"[4] packed there—to suggest the impossibility of what we expect from our writers—that they not only tell us stories, they also tell us how to live. She opens *The White Album* with that famous, portentous line. And then spends the whole book deconstructing the problems with that idea. While also, at least in my case, offering me a model I'd held up, as a way to learn how to live.

Joan had given me something I'd needed for ages—as a writer, as a human. A confident voice in my head, telling me that, no matter how dark things got, there was a way forward, even if it wasn't cute or nice, even if we didn't see it until years after the fact. Our story was our way forward. That was what I had done, with all of the pain and longing of my missing relationship with my father, what I had gotten down on the page in my book. But what would my story be, now, when only a few people cared to hear it? When no one clamored for my next book. When I had to keep finding new ways to demonstrate I was a writer, at least for myself (the only one doubting it, I suppose). When I had to keep finding ways to live.

My last tour stop was on Father's Day, by design. I'd been invited to take part in a monthly reading series, organized by a writer I liked and admired. It was a small but warm event, and my book had landed me a spot on its stage. I was grateful, as I had been for each and every reader who found my book, especially those

I'd met on tour that shared with me bits of their own troubled relationships with their dads. I valued these connections, at the same time that I had difficulty accepting there really wouldn't be more of them.

Looking back, I can see I was a person doing the best I could with where I was at, and how much pain I was still in—enough that I couldn't organize it, or hide it. Even though I was supposed to be the expert, now, reporting back from the other side of the abyss, on where we were heading, I lacked Joan's cool analysis. I lacked her dry wit. More than anything, I lacked her aloofness, and reading her books was not enough to impart it to me.

Of course, now, a few years older and a few bruises wiser, I can also see that, deeper down, Joan is confessing to her own case of imposter syndrome, even though, as far as I'd been concerned, Joan had made it, rife as her piece is with details like: "in the first-class cabins of the planes on which we traveled,"[5] and in conversations with the "*Daily News* photographer who was taking my picture."[6] And she's exposing her own interrogation of the sanity of our insistence in seeking wisdom from her at all— one harried writer, traveling with her young daughter, who finally confesses in her final appearance, and her final line: "I don't know where we're heading…but I'm heading home."[7]

Ironically, though, it was only by publishing my first book, and standing up for its stories, again and again, even when it felt like no one was listening, that I finally reached the other side, the place from which I can look back.

Maybe Joan is not comfortable being the oracle pop culture wants her to be. Maybe she was finally forced to solve this problem for herself when she, too, became an oracle of herself in the beloved, deeply personal, grief memoirs she has published in the latter half of her career. Maybe that's the whole point—we can all only be responsible for our own little plots of personhood. But she—and all writers—do matter, even if culture has moved on. They remain our oracles, our traveling companions, during our own dark nights of the soul—which, in my case, was my own last step on the road to becoming a writer. Period. Full stop. Becoming, in a sense, an oracle of myself—a person for whom the stories of my own life did in fact give me some idea of how to live, no matter who—if anyone—cared to listen.

Endnotes:

1. Joan Didion, "On the Road," in *The White Album* (New York: Farrar, Straus and Giroux, 1979), 175.
2. Didion, "On the Road," 173.
3. Didion, "On the Road," 175.
4. Didion, "On the Road," 175.
5. Didion, "On the Road," 176.
6. Didion, "On the Road," 178.
7. Didion, "On the Road," 179.

Why I Don't Answer the Phone:
A Conversation with Joan Didion about Self-Respect

By Linda Immediato

IN 1961, JOAN DIDION was asked to pinch-hit a piece for *Vogue*. The issue was going to press, and another writer had failed to turn their story in on time. The topic was self-respect. Didion wrote not just to a word count but an exact character count. As a journalist, I can attest this is no slap shot. But for me the harder task would be taking on the subject matter itself. What do I know about self-respect? I have often found myself berating myself for doing something that no self-respecting person would do. What does self-respect look like? Where does it come from? Joan begins her piece, "Once, in a dry season, I wrote in large letters across two pages of a notebook that innocence ends when one is stripped of the delusion that one likes oneself."[1]

Did I like myself? When I'm in need of an honest assessment of my life, I clean my bedroom. I take an inventory of objects I've acquired and the things I've neglected to do. It only seems fair to look those shameful bales of dust and dander that have collected in unattended corners square in the eye. So what did I discover? Along with the tumbleweeds of pet hair, I realized that I might be in danger of becoming a hoarder. And the worst kind—a sneaky hoarder. I have over the course of several months become adept at finding places to stash things, places that are not always in my eyeline. I deviously hid things in so many spots, scattering the embarrassment, distributing it in a way that no one could guess its true mass. With palpable anxiety, I pulled these things out from under the dresser, from behind the nightstand, and from carelessly stacked piles on the bookshelf. What was I hoarding? A lot of reusable shopping bags, they give them away like they're free these days. I have more shopping totes than paper bags. Which brings up a horrible thought: What if all of the paper bags are simply replaced by these manufactured ones and the world fills up with crudely made, logo emblazoned carryalls? I worry about this despite the fact that I often forget to bring a bag and have to buy one, sometimes two to double bag it. I didn't like that about myself. Nor did I like seeing Christmas cards that were never sent, never even addressed. One of them read "New Year's Resolution #1: Send More Mail to My Friends and Family Telling Them I Love Them." Pitiful.

I didn't like the fact that the awesome Neil deGrasse Tyson paper doll my friend Red gave me for my birthday sat un-DIY'ed by me. I love Neil deGrasse Tyson. I binge-watched his show *Cosmos*. I go to the planetarium in NYC at least once every year. My religious beliefs are in line with his! I love my friend Red, who knew I would like a Neil deGrasse Tyson paper doll, procured it, wrapped it up, and gave it to me for my birthday. So why? Why is Neil deGrasse Tyson lying, two dimensionally, in his skivvies under a fine film of dust, sandwiched between the as-yet-to-be framed wine label my sister gave me off the bottle of the Take it Easy Eagles cabernet we shared last year, and a coffee-stained copy of *Because of Bernard*, a half-completed screenplay.

No, I'm not liking myself very much right now. I am shrinking from life. The sound of a phone ringing fills me with dread. It has become the symbol, the foreboding reminder of all of the things I've yet to do, forgot to do, am scared to do, or too lazy to do. Like that screenplay...Isn't that why I moved to Los Angeles? To become a screenwriter? What happened to that dream? Nobody with a shred of self-respect abandons their dreams.

But Joan says to be cautious of misplaced self-respect. For her, not being elected to Phi Beta Kappa marked the end of her innocence. About the rejection she writes, "To such doubtful amulets had my self-respect been pinned, and I faced myself that day with the nonplussed wonder of someone who has come across a vampire and found no garlands of garlic at hand."[2]

That vampire came for me and I found myself similarly without a garland of garlic. I was thirty years old, living in Venice with my twenty-year-old boyfriend. Eight months earlier I was living in New York City with my best friend Sara, an actress. My first screenplay had just been optioned by a well-known director. The contract was signed, the check sent, the chunk of money sitting in my bank account. And with the dastardly mix of naivete and bravado most commonly seen in someone at least a decade younger, I quit my editor's job at *Gourmet* magazine and booked a one-way ticket to Los Angeles. I was scared to death to leave New York, the place I had lived since birth. But Sara promised she would join me in a couple of months. To psyche ourselves up, we held "visualization exercises" while looking in the mirror. We pantomimed driving Thelma and Louise-style down tree-lined Sunset Boulevard, waving to fans and giving a what's up to fellow

A-list celebrities. "Hey, Clooney!" we would coyly shout while pretending to steer the convertible. I dreamed of living in Laurel Canyon, in a Case Study house with a view and a pool.

I flew to LA on January 19, 2004, rented a room in a house in West Hollywood with my own bathroom. It had a marble tub with Jacuzzi jets that could seat four, if you were into that sort of thing. Turned out the Jacuzzi jets didn't work, but regardless, back then I really thought I had arrived. I rented a red convertible sports car...by the week. I plowed through the option money like I was somebody's trophy wife. Months passed and Sara never came. The LA guy I had been seeing long distance dumped me. And the money was running out. Six months. The director said I'd be on a movie set in six months. At which point I'd get the remainder of my chunk of change, and how big that chunk was depended on who produced it and with what budget. Either way it was a good chunk of change.

I had met Adonis, the twenty-year-old, technically then nineteen, during the salad days. The days when I still had cash flow, when I could burn through time without a worry in the world. LA was brand-new and everything was still possible. Adonis and I hooked up at my first Coachella. We watched the Pixies play and everything was electric, neon-bright. Adonis clung to me so tightly we melted together under the merciless Indio sun. For absolutely no reason at all I went to the Cannes Film Festival a few days later, and there are few things that will be etched as deeply in my mind as the sight of the tan, cherubic Adonis waiting for me beside his 1964 sun-faded blue Lincoln Continental convertible, with a white lily in his hand, outside the baggage claim at LAX. Also inked in the recesses of my memory are the days when, with nothing else to do, he and I hung out at his aunt's place, a cottage right off the boardwalk in Venice.

We would walk barefoot, hand in hand. He would lead and I would follow, anywhere, watching the sun kiss his unblemished skin, and wrap a glowing halo around his surfer locks. As all of the LA clichés I dreamt of manifested themselves, Adonis looked down at me, with all the sincerity of a boy who has yet to become a man, and said, "You're so rad."

A few months later the money had run out. The vampire had finally shown his face. I was going to have to get a job if I was going to have any self-respect at all. And I did. I waited tables in a fancy-schmancy restaurant on Abbot Kinney. At the end of my first day on the job I locked myself in the bathroom and cried. The scent of patchouli incense, which was endlessly burned by the owner's decree, will always smell less musky and more bittersweet to me. I chided myself for being so foolish to give up a good gig and move across the country. *Gourmet* was a national magazine, a Conde Nast publication for Christ's sake. I had my own office, and outside the door was a little plaque with my name—in Helvetica or some other sans serif font—on it. Just a few floors down from *Vogue*! And here I was, working the brunch shift again.

Eventually, a journalist quit at one of the few LA-based publications, and I got the job. I cut my teeth at the *LA Weekly*. To this day it's the best job I ever had. I wrote my first cover story for the *LA Weekly*. It was a profile of an architect. Sara had finally moved to LA from New York and she was living with me and Adonis. She refused to read my cover story, gently tossing the paper aside while glaring, "You didn't come to LA to become a journalist again!"

Since then, I've bounced from publication to publication, but always her words come back to haunt me: "You didn't come to LA to become a journalist again!"

No, Sara, I did not.

But I think of Leonard Cohen's song "The Traitor," which in the documentary *I'm Your Man* he says is about "betraying some mission we feel we were mandated to fulfill. And being unable to fulfill it and coming to the understanding that the real mandate was not to fill it. And that the deeper courage was to stand guiltless in the predicament in which you found yourself."[3] So I may chime in with you from time to time and call myself a traitor. But I know it's only some misplaced self-respect.

◆◆◆

I WENT THROUGH THIS phase a few years ago…I called it "fucking with Craigslist": posting something just to see what came back, if anything at all. I put up a post on the lost and found section stating that I had lost my self-respect and if anyone should find it, I sure would like it back, or at the very least, tell me where I could find a new one. I included a few clues as to where I might have lost it. I described a tawdry encounter I had after the Adonis breakup. The incident involved a couple of airplane-size bottles of wine, a playground, and a parked Toyota Corolla. I received two responses, one, very angry, and clearly from the person in that anecdote, for he venomously described far too many details, including which street the Toyota Corolla was parked on. The world is just too small for Craigslist. The other reply was from a total stranger, at least I like to think so, and it read: "You don't need a new one…I like the old one. Embrace your life, some people never live once."

Didion says self-respect has nothing to do with the approval of others, nor is it "some kind of charm against snakes, something that keeps those who have it locked away in some unblighted Eden, out of strange beds."[4]

The relationship with Adonis didn't last, although we tried one more time to make it work, ten years later. But the journalism stuck. It opened the city up to me, a place that was so foreign, vast and seemingly impenetrable, each assignment emboldening me to uncover the secrets it kept as I told the stories of its inhabitants. I wrote about the musicians and artists who immortalize it, the architects who build its very foundations, fashion designers who solidify LA's place as the epicenter of style. I covered politics and gave a voice to the voiceless and powerless.

Years before I moved to LA, it was journalists like Didion who painted the portrait of the city for me. I remember commuting on the subway as I read her description of the rapture of Los Angeles's freeways. It all sounded so exotic to me. Even now, decades later, her words often filter through my mind when I'm trying to find the rhythm of lane changes.

And as I waded through the detritus of my life I discovered a pile of my old clippings. I sat on the floor and pored through them. I thought of all the work that went into them—the late nights on deadline, the countless times I had to miss out on a friend's party or an A-list-studded publicity event because the clock was ticking and there were typos to fix and clever headlines to write. Putting out each issue felt like going to war; my coworkers and I were soldiers in the trenches, and the pressure created the kind of close camaraderie that many won't ever experience at their jobs. Lifelong friendships were born.

I realized that this *is* what I came to LA to do.

As I said, if you want to give yourself back to yourself, the best way to start is by cleaning your room.

ENDNOTES:

1. Joan Didion, "Self-Respect: Its Source, Its Power," in *Vogue*, August 1, 1961, 62. https://www.vogue.com/article/joan-didion-self-respect-essay-1961

2. Didion, "Self-Respect: Its Source, Its Power," 62.

3. Leonard Cohen, *I'm Your Man*, DVD, directed by Lian Lunson (2005; Lions Gate Entertainment).

4. Didion, "Self-Respect: Its Source, Its Power," 63.

A Letter to Joan on Turning Fifty-Five

By Tracy McMillan

DEAR JOAN DIDION,

I'm writing to you because I have recently become middle-aged. In Los Angeles. I'm not sure precisely when it happened. Not when I turned forty—I know that much. Because that's when I expected it to happen and I braced myself for an onslaught of oldness feelings, and then the birthday came and went, and then some months came, and went and finally the whole year came and went and still, I felt thirty-five. I will admit I was somewhat disappointed. But I just put on my size twenty-six jeans and went on about my life.

I should also tell you I was not that great of a young person. All young people are confused, and I was no exception—I got married at nineteen to an oil company executive, but went out almost every night with my age-appropriate friends—simultaneously the kind of young person who says yes to the "plastics" job in *The Graduate*, and the kind of young person like those rappers in a music video, whisking hundred-dollar bills off the top of a stack of hundred-dollar bills into life's metaphorical club. Not so much because I wanted to be a big spender or get someone to dance for me. More that I didn't care that much about hundred-dollar bills and all that whisking made me feel like I was doing something. As for my marriage, I truly loved to iron shirts.

I won't bore you with all the details of the intervening years, but let's just say no one was surprised when I found myself forty-two years old, living in a one-bedroom apartment, writing television news just enough to pay the rent, with a ten-year-old son, no health insurance, and three amicable divorces. (To my credit, I consider that last thing a legit achievement.) I was not one of those people who came to Los Angeles with a dream—to have a dream supposes you think something transcendent could happen in some realm, even if it's a realm where you're sleeping, and I didn't really think anything transcendent could happen to me anywhere, or ever. I was definitely not yet middle-aged during the One-Bedroom Apartment Years, but nevertheless I had arrived at a point where I was deeply in need of some inspiration.

And money.

Joan, that's when I discovered you. I mean, really discovered. I had heard of you, of course. But I didn't know what you were all about. A situation I sort of chalk up to being a Broadcast-Journalism major, instead of an English major—as well as a woman of color. (Two facts which, to my mind anyway, are not unrelated.) I had not yet read *The White Album*. I did not yet know about ignorant armies jostling in the night. I had not yet seen you standing in front of that Corvette.

And then, one day, I had.

Suddenly I knew why all those English majors had been talking about you all these years. Not just because you were a fatalist, and a beauty, and a teller of truth. But because you made

writing look and feel like rock and roll. And despite having
been in a band for a seven-year period we can loosely refer to
as My Band Phase (one of the details I won't bore you with), all
I had ever really wanted to be was a writer. All I had ever really
wanted to do was to have an idea and communicate it to another
human being—or maybe millions of them. Not because I wanted
to be a big spender, or get someone to dance for me. But because
I wanted to feel less alone. And I knew other people did, too.

So what does all this have to do with middle-aging in
Los Angeles? And why am I telling you about it? Well, that thing
you do for girls in college—Joan, you did for me in my forties.
In "On Keeping a Notebook," you said, "We are well advised to
keep on nodding terms with the people we used to be, whether
we find them attractive company or not. Otherwise they…come
hammering on the mind's door at 4:00 a.m. of a bad night and
demand to know who deserted them, who betrayed them, who is
going to make amends."[1] I know you were talking about the selves
I might have been trying to put behind me, but the way I saw it,
it applied just as much (if not more) to the selves I could be, the
selves I was supposed to be, the selves I was failing to be by not
even trying.

And so, right about the time I should have been starting to
prepare for my obsolescence—because we all know Hollywood
has few good roles for women over forty—I improbably started
to hammer on my own door and make amends to myself. I wrote
a screenplay inspired by the demise of my third marriage. I got an
agent (somehow) and started taking Hollywood meetings, telling
all these nice Ivy League children about my drug-dealing dad and
my sex-working mother. Joan, you would have been proud. For
the first time ever, I dared to say what I really thought, even if it
might make some people mad, and I even said it in print. I took the

covenant between reader and writer to tell the truth and nothing but the truth—a covenant you mastered like no one else—and decided it should include the whole Internet. Because why not? After decades of playing small, I finally stopped whining, stopped complaining, worked harder, and spent more time alone. Just like you told me to.

The next thing I knew, I was writing television, had an essay go viral, got some book deals, wrote some books, did a TEDx thing, and became a person who goes on television and talks about relationships. I was embracing my inner you, Joan—if we had been born millennials. Because who are you if not the original influencer?

The years ticked by, and with them, the ages. Forty-eight, forty-nine, fifty, fifty-one. You would think Los Angeles is the kind of place you'd never want to grow oldish, due to all the palm trees and eyelash extensions. But who knows better than you they're just modern forms of Manifest Destiny—there to be embraced, not feared? I once heard someone say that up close, the beautiful things in Los Angeles are ugly, and the ugly things are beautiful. I always thought they meant that even the most stunning A-list actress has probably, at some point before collecting her Oscar, let a surgeon draw black lines on her face, then laid down on a table with an IV in her arm, counted backward from one hundred, and let a knife slice into her flesh in order to make a camera love her just a little bit more than it already does. Or conversely, that some of the best restaurants are in strip malls. But couldn't it just as easily also mean that here—and possibly only here—the most dreaded life stage could actually be the most thrilling?

In fact, Los Angeles might be the ideal place to be middle-aged. Not only are healthy food, Pilates, and Botox relatively cheap and plentiful—so are creative collaborators, sublime weather, and divorced people to fall in love with, some of them quite wonderful. And if you almost never eat carbs, you can even still wear size twenty-six jeans.

Which brings me to the purpose of my letter. I want to thank you, Joan. Assuming nothing drastic happens between now and then, by the time you read this, I will have turned fifty-five. Now that is a fairly big number—way past the middle of my life, if we're honest—more like the very, very, very beginning of the end. I may not be precisely sure when middle age happened—Was it the meeting with the estate lawyer? The problem with my knees? My son's college graduation? But it doesn't matter, because I am most definitely here. But I'm not scared. In fact, I'm exhilarated. Thanks to you.

Yes, you.

Sometimes when people ask me about my empty nest I say it's like being twenty-eight, without the anxiety. Back then, I wanted to know: *What was going to happen? Would I ever have kids? What about a career? Where would I live? Would I ever be happy?* It was, let's be real, excruciating. But now, time has told. Everything turned out. And you were, in fact, the perfect role model. Everything you promised I could be, I am. I got the career, I got the baby, I got allll the husbands. I even got California. The old me has turned into a young you. And I'm standing in front of a Corvette with my wrinkles, wearing a maxi dress. Ready to step on the gas.

ENDNOTES:

1. Joan Didion, "On Keeping a Notebook," in *Slouching Towards Bethlehem* (Farrar, Straus and Giroux, 1968), 139.

The Last Private Man:
From Howard Hughes
to Jeff Goldblum

By Dan Crane

"That we have made a hero out of Howard Hughes tells us something interesting about ourselves...tells us that the secret point of money and power in America is neither the things that money can buy nor power for power's sake...but absolute personal freedom, mobility, privacy."[1]
—Joan Didion, "7000 Romaine, Los Angeles 38"

"Jeff's like a delicate flower. And we, his fans, are the sunlight that keeps him alive. He doesn't go out in the sun. The reason he's so tanned is from all the adoration."[2]
—Taiki Waititi, who directed Jeff Goldblum in *Thor: Ragnarok*

IT'S A CLOUDLESS THURSDAY morning, and just after ten Jeff Goldblum answers his door, shirtless.

"Helloooo," he says, drawing out the "o" and then letting it fall in his devious, bemused, and characteristically Goldblumian fashion. He speaks slowly, sexily. "Let me put some clothes on and then I'll be ready to go." He sizes up the singer of my band (a woman in her early twenties), grabs her hand, and flirtatiously remarks, "This'll be fun! I'll be right back…" He vanishes like a vapor down the hall.

We are at Jeff Goldblum's house to shoot a music video for our band because the man who manages Jeff Goldblum's jazz group also happens to run a small record label that puts out our music. We begged him to ask Jeff Goldblum to be in the video as I've been politely obsessed with Jeff Goldblum since moving to Los Angeles in 2004. In the past fifteen or so years, Jeff Goldblum has become the most interesting, best-dressed, most enviable, most worthy of imitation famous man in Hollywood. Why shouldn't he be in our video?

Naturally Jeff Goldblum said yes—not because he liked (or had probably even heard) our music, but because he is open to such things. Jeff Goldblum is *game*.

Jeff Goldblum has not chosen to hide behind tall Beverly Hills hedges and wear baseball hats, sunglasses, and sweats like most other Hollywood celebs (if you ever want to see a famous person in Hollywood, look for the person wearing a baseball hat, sunglasses, and sweats). Unlike the Howard Hughes of Didion's essay "7000 Romaine, Los Angeles 38"—"whose public appearances are now less frequent than those of The Shadow"[3]—Jeff Goldblum didn't become famous in order to hide. Jeff Goldblum is everywhere, and Jeff Goldblum is accessible.

Jeff Goldblum is the obverse of the superficial LA stereotype. If Howard Hughes was the "last private man, the dream we no longer admit,"[4] then Jeff Goldblum might be the last public man—or at least the public man's apotheosis. It's 2019, and despite society's widely acknowledged death of privacy, Jeff Goldblum warmly, knowingly embraces his lack thereof.

Jeff Goldblum is what you want LA to be. For most, LA disappoints: true celebrities are ghosts hermetically residing in mansions behind twenty-foot-high ficuses seeking Hughesian levels of privacy; but Jeff Goldblum is a party, and you're invited. He is the *celebration* in celebrity.

Like the Hughes of Didion's essay, everyone in LA has a Jeff Goldblum story—and if they don't, one's certainly not challenging to obtain.

Jeff Goldblum is playing jazz most every Wednesday evening at a small club in Los Feliz. Do you want your picture taken with Jeff Goldblum? Come to the show! It's fun, the music is good (if you tolerate jazz), and Jeff Goldblum plays trivia games with the audience between songs. Often the games become a variation on "Six Degrees of Kevin Bacon"—name any actor, and Jeff Goldblum will quickly find a path to Jeff Goldblum via other actors in other movies. What Jeff Goldblum wants you to know is that he's been in a lot of movies (according to IMDB, his first of over 125 film and television credits was playing "Freak #1" in 1974's *Death Wish*). And he knows everybody. And everybody loves Jeff Goldblum. Just like you do. After the second set, around 11:30 p.m., Jeff Goldblum hangs around until anyone who desires a selfie with him has an iPhone chock full of snaps. The photos will quickly be Instagrammed and hashtagged and garner numerous likes. I know, I've posted one!

"You look like a…young Bob Dylan," Jeff Goldblum said to me once several years ago when I volunteered to sing "I've Got You Under My Skin" at his jazz gig—back when it was more of a karaoke kind of thing. I didn't sound like Bob Dylan. As I recall, I was quite drunk, forgot the words, and sounded horrendous.

Jeff Goldblum makes you feel good by always calling you the "young version" of a famous person. Jeff Goldblum says you look like a young version of a famous person because he wants you to feel what it's like to be famous. When you meet or get your picture taken with or see Jeff Goldblum play jazz, you become fame adjacent. *You have a Jeff Goldblum story!* You become one of Didion's Hollywood denizens who "once processed fan photographs, say, or knew Jean Harlow's manicurist."[5]

You also provide an answer to the question, why is Jeff Goldblum doing this? Why not use your wealth and fame to seclude yourself behind a ficus? Because money can't buy adulation.

"You look like a young…Bert Convy," Jeff Goldblum said another time he spotted me in the audience at his jazz gig. (Bert Convy, if you don't recall, was a frequent guest on the *Love Boat*. He had wavy dark hair and was always a hit with the ladies). I was honored.

"You look like a young El Topo," Jeff Goldblum said to me the last time I was in the audience at his jazz gig. (*El Topo*, if you've never seen it, was the titular character played by Alejandro Jodorowsky in a Mexican acid Western film which *The New York Times* called "a very strange masterpiece."[6]) A few weeks later, I dressed up as El Topo for Halloween. One person got it.

Jeff Goldblum loves playing dress-up and cannot be discussed without referencing his style. "Who is the male fashion icon for now? Jeff Goldblum, of course,"[7] noted *The Guardian* in 2018, the same year *Vanity Fair* raved, "Jeff Goldblum's Style Is a Pure Shot of Joy."[8] A 2017 profile in *GQ* noted, "Goldblum has hipper tastes than guys half his age. And when he stocks up on clothes at places like Just One Eye—a high-end concept shop as eccentric as he is— he wears suitably stylish clothes, like this Bottega Veneta jacket."[9]

The address of the "high-end concept shop" Just One Eye? Yes, that's right, 7000 Romaine.

Today, the art deco former headquarters of eccentric millionaire Howard Hughes houses an upscale couture boutique. If you're a celebrity looking to (conspicuously) hide from the paparazzi and the hoi polloi, at Just One Eye you can find the whole uniform at suitably absurd prices: a Gucci LA Angels baseball cap is $590, and OAMC "drawcord pants" (aka sweatpants) are $720. Green-lensed aviators go for around $1,000.

Or, if you're Jeff Goldblum, you'll be gifted a blue floral-print Prada shirt that features gray faux-fur shoulders, pose in it for a photo posted to your 1.7 million Instagram followers, and caption it, "Silverback gorilla, but make it fashion?" Jeff Goldblum knows his shirt is ridiculous, but he doesn't care. Jeff Goldblum is in on the joke.

In the end, we got the shot we needed for our music video: Wearing a white T-shirt with random letters printed on it, Jeff Goldblum opens his door, we hand him a pamphlet, and then he feeds the pamphlet to his Instagram-famous ginger poodle named Woody Allen. He holds our young female singer's hand for just a second too long, and then we move on. To rephrase Didion, he is the last public man, the dream we love to admit.

ENDNOTES:

1. Joan Didion, "7000 Romaine, Los Angeles 38," in *Slouching Towards Bethlehem* (New York: Farrar, Strauss and Giroux, 1968), 71.
2. Anna Peele, "The World According to Jeff Goldblum," *GQ*, November 1, 2017, https://www.gq.com/story/jeff-goldblum-the-oral-history.
3. Didion, "7000 Romaine, Los Angeles 38," 68.
4. Didion, "7000 Romaine, Los Angeles 38," 72.
5. Didion, "7000 Romaine, Los Angeles 38," 67.
6. Peter Schjeldahl, "Should 'El Topo' Be Elevated To 'El Tops'?" *The New York Times*, June 6, 1971, https://www.nytimes.com/1971/06/06/archives/should-el-topo-be-elevated-to-el-tops.html.
7. Hadley Freeman, "Who is the male fashion icon for now? Jeff Goldblum, of course," *The Guardian*, July 11, 2018, https://www.theguardian.com/fashion/2018/jul/11/who-is-the-male-fashion-icon-for-now-jeff-goldblum.
8. Kenzie Bryant, "Jeff Goldblum's Style Is a Pure Shot of Joy," *Vanity Fair*, September 11, 2018, https://www.vanityfair.com/style/2018/09/jeff-goldblum-style-evolution.
9. Peele, "The World According to Jeff Goldblum."

Points on a Map

By Steph Cha

THE LAST SUNDAY BEFORE we were married, in September 2013, my husband Matt and I spent an afternoon apartment hunting with my friend June. We were living in Los Feliz at the time, and June was looking to move out of her childhood home in Hancock Park, a Spanish-style house on Citrus Avenue. I wanted her to be as close to me as possible.

When we were younger—June and I went to middle school and high school together—I always thought of June as my friend who was in the center of things. I grew up in Encino, in a cul-de-sac on a hill in the suburbs, but Koreatown was in Koreatown, so my family spent a lot of time eating and shopping and hanging with my grandmother in Central Los Angeles. That's where June lived, near the Koreatown Plaza, but also near Larchmont and the Grove, just a few minutes in the car to get to all the places that seemed to define the city for a child of the Valley.

I left LA for college, but whenever I was home, June took me to hip restaurants and parties in parking lots, to Cinespace and Cinespia. She was in fashion school at Otis and knew where to go.

I still remember the mix CD she made me for Christmas in eighth grade, in the brief window between my K-pop phase and my God rock phase, with a track list that included both Portishead and The Chordettes. It was June who first introduced me to the part of LA I eventually came to know as an adult, when I moved back home after seven years away for school. She took me to Silver Lake (the red-lit Cha Cha Lounge, where we drank sugary cocktails and took pictures in a photo booth), Los Feliz (Fred 62 on Vermont, a street I thought I knew because it ran through K-Town), and Echo Park (a Rilo Kiley concert at The Echo, which freaked out my mom, who went to high school in Los Feliz in the 1970s when Echo Park was still gritty, before vamoosing to the burbs).

When I wrote my first book, an LA mystery novel inspired, of course, by Raymond Chandler, I wanted to write down the Los Angeles I knew, to make it feel real, even mappable, a story that might have happened on familiar streets. I remember the pleasurable jolts of recognition I got while reading *The Big Sleep* for the first time, as a college freshman who had somehow never read a novel about her own city, and I wanted to recreate that feeling for someone else. It might have been a similar impulse that drove Joan Didion to devote the last third of *Slouching Towards Bethlehem* to "Seven Places of the Mind," seven essays that comprise (among many, many other things) a meditation on location. One of these essays even includes latitude and longitude coordinates in the title ("Letter from Paradise, 21' 19' N., 157' 52' W"); and "Los Angeles Notebook" talks about Chandler, quoting his famous words on the Santa Ana winds. I am aware, each time I dare mention a hot, dry wind, that I am writing in both of their shadows, trying to find my place within the same territory.

It is possible to take this task too literally. When Matt read an early draft of my first book, he told me I'd gone too hard on the Google Maps, and he was right—there was no need to include driving directions every time my protagonist got in her car. But I used real places whenever I could—I'd been to them, and I felt that gave me the authority I needed to write them— and in many cases, specified addresses that really didn't need to be specified.

June's house on Citrus played a significant role. It was home to two of my major characters, and the very first murder I wrote—one of a dozen or so murders I've written in my career as a crime writer—took place in the street out front. I got June's permission to use her house, but when she read the book, she was still a little unsettled—she hadn't realized I was planning to include her actual address, or that I'd be staging a strangulation in the dark street only yards away from where she watched TV and ate breakfast.

When she decided it was time to move out (unrelated, though it was within months of my book's release) and find an apartment, Matt and I helped her sift through listings and drive through Los Feliz looking for vacancies. Matt was the one who found the apartment on Waverly Drive: a spacious, rent-controlled one-bedroom in a 1970s building on a quiet street, tucked into a hill above Rowena, one of the calmer thru-ways of the neighborhood.

June moved in and made it her home: it was her first apartment, her first time living away from her parents, and she furnished the place tastefully, artfully; she amassed books and bottles of alcohol, hosted elegant parties. She found a new rhythm, made new friends, and enjoyed the freedom of life in LA with a place of her own.

I remember when June soured on that place. She said she'd grown tired of the eerie sleepiness of her street; there was an old man who sat in a red car in front of the building, staring creepily at passersby, occasionally playing trumpet. But what she told me first was that she'd gotten in an Uber earlier that week and that her driver had asked her, as he drove her away from her apartment at night, if she knew about the murders on Waverly.

◆◆◆

FOR TWO YEARS, JUNE had been living down the street from the house at 3301 Waverly Drive, where the Manson Family slaughtered Leno and Rosemary LaBianca on August 9, 1969. This was the evening after the Tate murders, which Joan Didion learned about earlier that day, "sitting in the shallow end of my sister-in-law's swimming pool in Beverly Hills,"[1] in the same zip code, most likely, as the house rented by Sharon Tate and Roman Polanski, where the murders of Tate and four others took place. Didion wrote about the fallout from the Manson murders in "The White Album," her sprawling, shimmering essay about LA in the 1960s that helped define the era and famously marked its end: "Many people I know in Los Angeles," she wrote, "believe that the sixties ended abruptly on August 9, 1969, ended at the exact moment when word of the murders on Cielo Drive traveled like brushfire through the community."[2]

Almost fifty years later, disturbed by the proximity of the LaBianca house, disturbed as well by the male Uber driver who decided to tell her about the murders in detail, even as she asked him to stop, June moved out of her apartment on Waverly Drive— built, incidentally, in 1970, just after the actual end of the 1960s— into an old house on Kensington Road in Echo Park, which she rented with roommates. The revelation had made her own street feel creepy and haunted, a place she no longer wanted to live.

Of course, there have been countless other violent crimes in Los Angeles over the last fifty years. If June had checked the

Los Angeles Times Homicide Report, as I just did, she might have learned that a twenty-one-year-old man was shot and killed on her new block on April 8, 2012. The Homicide Report maps murder in Los Angeles, naming and counting the (as of May 2019) 16,591 people killed by homicide in the County since 2000. One of those victims was shot across the street from the park where Matt and I walk our dogs. One of those victims was my cousin, a crazy thing that is maybe not so crazy—after all, most of those victims must have had cousins.

This is a part of living in Los Angeles, or really in any big city: Life is dense here—you're always close to other people, bumping up against their history, their culture, their violence. Do you know what I see when I read Joan Didion, or for that matter, Raymond Chandler, or Walter Mosley, or Michael Connelly? I see a map overlaid on my map of Los Angeles. When Didion, in the essay "In Hollywood," tells a New Yorker complaining about the Polo Lounge that "people who live and work here do not frequent hotel bars either before or after dinner,"[3] it pleases me that Matt and I went just once, when we stayed at the Beverly Hills Hotel for an in-town wedding that fell on our first anniversary in 2014, and that it was only us and an old man sucking face with a young woman, almost certainly a prostitute.

Between 1966 and 1971, during the years depicted in "The White Album," Didion lived in a giant house on Franklin Avenue that has since become a New Agey spiritual center. The house is a straight shot, less than four miles, from the first apartment Matt and I shared, just north of the intersection of Franklin and Rodney Drive. Franklin Avenue! I lit up when I saw that, because when I read writers I love writing about Los Angeles, I look for our shared geographies, linking us across time; I savor these recognitions as if they might tie us together.

Los Angeles is an enormous place—it's hardly significant that one person lived here, and that fifty years later, someone else did, too. Significant is Didion knowing Sharon Tate and sharing a godchild with Roman Polanski, then picking out Linda Kasabian's clothing for her testimony in Tate's murder trial, at the request of prosecutor Vincent Bugliosi. But Didion failed to draw conclusions from any of this. "In this light all connections were equally meaningful, and equally senseless,"[4] she wrote.

Probably, it doesn't mean anything that I once lived almost four miles from a place where Joan Didion lived in the 1960s. After all, what else is within four miles of any of us in Los Angeles at any given time? How many homes? How many people? How many crimes? But maybe that's what I'm getting at here, that all of us live among gruesome and spectacular events, among shiny and nasty people. To be a point on a map is common, universal, and therefore trivial. It is also to share a common universe, to lay claim to the extraordinary and the unimaginable.

Endnotes:

1. Joan Didion, "The White Album," *The White Album* (New York: Simon & Schuster, 1979), 41.
2. Didion, "The White Album," 46.
3. Joan Didion, "In Hollywood," *The White Album* (New York: Simon & Schuster, 1979), 156.
4. Didion, "The White Album," 43.

Waiting for Jim:
A Response to "The White Album"

By Caroline Ryder

MY FIRST SUMMER IN Los Angeles I was in my twenties, a young newspaper reporter from London, determined to woo the city, learn her words, her rules, her pleasures. I knew some of her myths—Jim Morrison and his black vinyl pants, for example— but I had yet to encounter Raymond Chandler's *The Long Goodbye*, Nathanael West's *The Day of the Locust*, and the thorny bougainvillea that'll make your fingers bleed. I had yet to sit with a left-handed lover at Musso & Frank and watch him take the orange rind out of his martini, wondering if the city's capricious emotional tides would engineer a second encounter or just... terminate us.

July Fourth fireworks crackled over Hollywood and I got the feeling this was a special day, the kind friends and family share with one another. I had neither friends nor family around, so I ordered tequila delivery from Pink Dot and settled in for the night with a copy of *The White Album*, stretching my body out on the stained carpet of my one-bedroom apartment. I pored over

Didion, cool mom in sharp neutrals who gave form to my own unrest. I followed as she strolled listlessly ahead, an unblinking tour guide in sunny Hades, doula of catastrophic rebirth, pointing out the landmarks of limitless paranoia that crisscross the sprawling city grid whose cracked thoroughfares invite us to drive toward a terminus called Beauty. Love. Success. Something.

A few nights earlier, at a party, I met a woman in her late thirties. Well-established in the city, she took pity on me as I wandered around uselessly with my notepad. She wore white, drove a vintage car, and understood design. I still have a photo of her from that night, taken on one of those disposable cameras, her panties around her ankles as she peed on the corner of Franklin and Highland, urine trickling along concrete, signs of life in a heat wave. Afterward, I helped her home. "Read this," she said, handing me a book. *The White Album.*

In the essay of the same name, about twenty pages in, Didion writes about the day she found herself sitting on the vinyl floor of Sunset Sound, the recording studio on Sunset and Cherokee, visiting The Doors. "Missionaries of apocalyptic sex,"[1] she calls them. For hours and hours, Didion, the whole band, and their entourage, wait for Jim Morrison, lead singer, to arrive. Didion's leg goes to sleep. Ray Manzarek eats a hard-boiled egg.

(If Only Morrison Were Here Then We Could Do Some Vocals.)

(If Only Morrison Were Here Then We Could Just Be Groovy.)

"Unspecific tensions seemed to be rendering everyone in the room catatonic,"[2] Didion writes, and visions of my friend's pee rolling slowly past the Hollywood Bowl spring to mind, limitless and free, stoned and immaculate. She was my first friend in Los Angeles. She gave me this atlas of invisible topographies, a guidebook to a city where magic and agony lay heavy on the air. Where future hurts take seed in faded red carpets.

(Weird Scenes Inside Studio A.)

Jim Morrison finally arrives. And no one acknowledges him. For a whole hour. Sixty minutes, no one even says hi. How awkward is that? And how perfect. How groovy. How fucking sexy. An hour later, Jim speaks. Do you want to know what the first words out of his mouth are?

"It's an hour to West Covina."[3]

(No-one Here Gets Out Alive.)

"It's an hour to West Covina."

(The west is the best. The West Is the Best.)

Jim lights a match. He studies the flame awhile, before slowly, deliberately lowering it to the fly of his black vinyl pants. I wish she were here, my friend, who crouched low on Franklin Avenue. She waited and waited, fodder for black vinyl crotches and men who cannot love, until she could wait no more. Eventually, she drove east, back to Florida, back to the small town where she once dreamt of living like Joan Didion in Los Angeles.

Now I wait, too. For left-handed lovers. For dead bougainvillea plants to bloom again, that they may prick my skin and make it red. For Raymond Chandler to gumshoe up to my door so I can ask him, "Ray, why do the clocks stop in Los Angeles?"

"That's what happens in Studio A," he might say. "You're just waiting for Jim. Beauty. Love. Success. Something. The sun. Terminated."

ENDNOTES:

1. Joan Didion, "The White Album," *The White Album* (New York: Simon & Schuster, 1979), 21.
2. Didion, "The White Album," 23.
3. Didion, "The White Album," 24.

The Black Albums:
How Joan Didion and The Beatles Went Noir Together

By Joe Donnelly

"In their eyes there's something lacking
What they need's a damn good whacking"[1]
—"Piggies," George Harrison, *The Beatles* (aka "The White Album")

JOAN DIDION GOT ME to take The Beatles seriously.

I know what you're thinking—what kind of idiot didn't take The Beatles seriously? Well, the *me* kind of idiot. The kind who grew up with a young, hippie-ish mom and her older husband, my dad, who was a pretty straight-laced fella before meeting my mom.

Dad was a child of the Depression, a man of the 1950s and a Korean War vet (stateside) who hated the Army, but still liked Ike. Worked in pharmaceuticals for a bit until he had enough of the shady dealings in that biz. *Mad Men* stuff. Then, he knocked up my mom with my older brother, got married, and the hippie shit hit the fan.

There's no zealot like a convert, and I'd say by 1968 (a fateful year for these purposes) my dad was in deep. All at once, it seemed, he had excommunicated himself from the Catholic Church; was sporting long hair, turtlenecks, and beads; and was doing his best to tweak the polite sensibilities of our suburban, New Jersey neighbors.

He was so down with the revolution that on November 15, 1969, he and my mom dragged my older brother, our three-year-old sister, and me to DC for the largest antiwar demonstration in history. I remember "One, two, three, four...we hate this fucking war" and the fragrant fog of marijuana, which I realize, looking back, my mom and uncle were contributing to enthusiastically.

A couple of months later, my parents had determined the resistance wasn't winning and we packed up and moved to Ireland, which was then still in the dark ages and an odd and jarring place for longhaired, irreligious, bell-bottomed kids to suddenly find themselves. We returned to the states in 1975 after the war was over and Nixon was out of office. But no matter where we were, The Beatles were with us in constant rotation on my dad's playlist. Constant like if Alexa was my dad and my dad was stuck. Only not stuck on the great Beatles—not on the *Rubber Soul* or *Revolver* or...yes, "The White Album" Beatles—but on the *Sgt. Pepper's* and *Yellow Submarine* and *Magical Mystery Tour* Beatles. The hippie, psychedelic Beatles. And it never stopped, not even in the mid-1970s when we were back in the USA.

By then, I'd decided I hated hippie shit—even, or especially, the Beatles hippie shit. In fact, well into adulthood, I feared that if I heard even the opening bars of "Being For The Benefit of Mr. Kite" or "Fixing A Hole" I'd vomit.

You know who else hated hippie shit? That's right, Joan Didion hated hippie shit. Hippies were the tea leaves in which

Didion read the stupefied, inarticulate end of American self-governance—most explicitly in "Slouching Towards Bethlehem," the essay (and later collection) that followed in the wake of the Summer of Love. That decline was something she may have been fifty years too early in predicting.

◆◆◆

Most of the essays in *Slouching Towards Bethlehem* were written after Didion returned to California in 1964 with her husband, John Gregory Dunne, a raconteur journalist with mid-level Hollywood connections. Hollywood money was what beckoned, so it's not surprising that Didion didn't come back to her beloved Sacramento—all but unrecognizable to her by then if "Notes from a Native Daughter" from the same collection is to be believed. Instead, she took up residence in a shabby-chic house on Franklin Avenue just below Runyon Canyon.

Hollywood has been the well-documented demise of many a lofty literary figure, but not so Didion. She wasn't one of those yet, but found upon her return a city and state going through the sort of civic and cultural transformations Didion excels at explaining, or exploiting, depending on who you're asking and what time of day it is.

Either way, the *Slouching* collection came out in 1968 and the *Los Angeles Times* promptly named Didion one of its "Women of the Year," an honor it bestowed between 1950–1977 on some three hundred women "of concept and vision, who by outstanding achievement to their fields of endeavor, have created and produced improvements affecting all our lives."

It was an interesting choice for the *Times*. William Tuohy was about to win the Pulitzer Prize for his Vietnam War coverage and the thirty-three-year-old publisher, Otis Chandler, was undertaking an ambitious reformation of the paper in hopes of keeping up with a city that was quickly transitioning from its booster past to its future as the most cosmopolitan city in America. Perhaps by choosing Didion, the *Times* was signifying some affinity for the kind of gimlet eye Didion was training on her home state.

Didion tells us in "The White Album," the eponymous essay from her second collection of California-centric nonfiction, that her new zip code had a rep as a "senseless-killing neighborhood."[2] I doubt it. I had moved to the same neighborhood about three decades later at the tail end of the city's most murderous period and the biggest threats to the peace were aggressive hookers and the eggs-over-easy at the All American Burger. Today, homes like hers sell for millions.

But Didion, to paraphrase a writer friend, has a strong sensibility that tends to bend everything to its will. That sensibility has been rightly hailed for blazing a trail through the patriarchy, like Sherman's march to the sea, for generations of women to follow. But daring to dabble in postmodernist reportage and crashing the New Journalism sausage party wasn't, in my opinion, her biggest literary insurrection.

For that, I think we have to consider her appropriation of noir and, I'm afraid, turn to Mike Davis's venerable *City of Quartz* for a little context. In the first chapter, "Sunshine or Noir," Davis calls noir "that great anti-myth" and likens it to a "transformational grammar turning each charming ingredient of the booster's arcadia into its sinister equivalent."[3]

Didion was looking for a transformational grammar when she arrived in LA. She was no longer the ingenue who arrived in New York a fashion-mag intern, but a full-grown woman of thirty-one with a husband and an emergent jadedness kindled by her years in New York and her disappointment when her debut novel *Run River* failed to move the needle on her literary ambitions.

She was also growing disillusioned with her own history. It's worth remembering that Didion was once an earnest and somewhat ingenuous girl who took the Manifest Destiny narratives of her childhood to heart. These "crossing" stories weren't just pages in secondary-school history books to her, they were family stories and oral traditions going back to the American Revolution.

Soon after she settled in Los Angeles she penned "Notes from A Native Daughter," which could have as easily been titled "Goodbye To All That BS." In it, Didion serves divorce papers on the stories she'd been saddled with since her youth—the ones about her plucky, pioneer forebears who won the West. It wasn't them, of course; it was big railroad, timber, mining, and agricultural concerns and the political apparatus they put in place to subsidize the larceny. Her people may have endured and done brutal things to get here, but they were bit players in the larger story.

In the late spring of 1967, Didion helicoptered into San Francisco's Haight-Ashbury on assignment for the *Saturday Evening Post*. She was meant to translate the hippie movement, which had been getting a lot of gee-whiz coverage, for the amusement of the squares back East. Instead, in the bright and cynical confines of her Los Angeles home, she wrote her classic end-of-the-1960s eulogy, "Slouching Towards Bethlehem," with its indelible first line: "The center wasn't holding."[4]

We can argue about whether or not the tiny fraction of the population represented by the lost children of Haight-Ashbury are an apt portent of the apocalypse, but what's for sure is that Didion was growing increasingly suspicious of narrative—both her own and the culture's—and its power over human discernment. So, what do we do when the stories we tell aren't up to the task of explaining things, or even providing an accurate framework for explaining things, but instead may be doing a disservice?

If you're Didion, you turn to the transformational grammar and counter narratives of noir. Her genius was taking noir fiction's "tough-guy" realism, as Davis puts it, out of its dusky, male-centric corner and using it as a weapon in her journalism. With it, she set about eviscerating the facile New California of political ingenues, exurban status seekers, schemers, hucksters and, most pointedly, dippy hippies. Without losing her distinctive woman's voice, Didion opened up noir's toolbox for generations of female (and male) journalists to use on those "bright, guilty" places Davis describes. For me, this is one of her most enduring contributions.

◆◆◆

"Well don't you know that happiness (happiness)
is a warm gun (is a warm gun, yeah)."[5]

—"Happiness Is a Warm Gun," John Lennon,
from *The Beatles* (aka "The White Album")

I WASN'T AWARE THAT Didion was a former neighbor when I got my $650-per-month street-level apartment with a window onto the parking lot back in the day. I wasn't a Didion aficionado, either. But at some point, I found myself confronting the kind of existential alienation Los Angeles inevitably confronts newcomers with. I took comfort in coffee; cigarettes; the dusty, sun-drenched hardwood floors; and *The White Album*.

I'm not sure how *The White Album* got in my hands, but it was probably on my arriviste reading list, along with *City of Quartz* and *Ask The Dust*—as inevitable a rite of passage as the alienation itself. But I do remember being as intrigued by Didion's persona as her prose. I was a journalist, after all, and she was managing to do what even Tom Wolfe couldn't, as much as he tried: she made journalism feel rock-star cool. In that, she became aspirational.

When she mined the lingua franca designation for the Beatles 1968 album for the title of her *White Album* collection, I wondered what it signified. Why didn't she call it *White Light/ White Heat,* for instance? What was I missing?

A *New York Times* profile accompanying the release of *The White Album* notes that Didion found *The Beatles* "ominous and disturbing, an album inextricably linked to the Manson Murders and the dissonance of the 1960s."[6] I hadn't thought about the Beatles as ominous or disturbing. Or had I? I started to remember how when "I Am The Walrus" and "A Day In The Life" seeped under our childhood bedroom doors late at night, the sound felt unsettling, different from the lullabies "All You Need Is Love" or "Octopus's Garden."

Turns out the Beatles' "White Album" was the band's own document of disillusionment and dread. It came after the group had tried to extend the summer of love by decamping to India for a meditation retreat in early 1968 with Maharishi Mahesh Yogi— "Sexy Sadie" as John Lennon would call him in song.

Also retreating were Mia Farrow, her sister Prudence, whose penchant for following rules was immortalized in "Dear Prudence," Donovan and Mike Love, whom history seems to indicate may have benefited the least from the yogi's ministrations, but who did help McCartney parody his band in "Back In The USSR."

Anyway, the lads weren't long for the door. Ringo bolted first, fed up with the vegan fare. McCartney, who supposedly tired of the holy man's obsequiousness, departed soon after Ringo with the glib sign-off: "I'm a new man!" Mike Love and Mia Farrow buggered out early, too, the latter stating in her autobiography that she felt "overwhelmed" by Maharishi's attention to her.

John hung in there longer, but hell hath no fury like a scorned Lennon. Before leaving, he composed his takedown of "Sexy Sadie," as well as the suicidal lament "Yer Blues," which he wrote when he realized that what he felt most in India was loneliness.

George, whose "It's All Too Much," is as enthusiastic an ode to Haight-Ashbury hippie girls as you can find and whose idea the whole Maharishi thing seems to have been, caught serious flak from his bandmates. Abandoned in India, he retreated back to the English countryside to write the sardonic rebuttals "While My Guitar Gently Weeps" and "Piggies."

The Beatles' "White Album" is an unruly mess of styles and syncopations. It's the sound of the band's own divorce from narrative. It has no center, no *Sgt. Pepper* to guide us, nor any *Magical Mystery Tour* to take us on. Instead, it has George's wobbly, nauseous guitar lines, John's happy, warm guns, and Paul's helter skelter. It's an album of violence, resignation, and fragmentation with a few moments of respite sprinkled in. It sounds like madness and, I realized late in life, it's the soundtrack to the atomization and social hemorrhaging Didion had been going on about.

"The White Album" is the Beatles *noir*. When you listen to it—I should say when you hear it—almost everything before and after it seems like child's play. No wonder Didion copped its name. It's almost like she wrote it.

The Beatles are once again in constant rotation in my house, thanks in no small part to Didion leading me back there. My five-year-old daughter loves the lullabies—"Octopus's Garden," "Yellow Submarine" and the like, but I know it's only a matter of time before she, too, discovers the White Albums.

ENDNOTES:

1. The Beatles, "Piggies," Track Four, Side Two, on *The Beatles,* Apple Records, 1968, vinyl LP.

2. Joan Didion, "The White Album," in *The White Album* (New York: Simon & Schuster, 1979), 15.

3. Mike Davis, *City of Quartz* (London: Verso, 1990), 37-38.

4. Joan Didion, "Slouching Towards Bethlehem," in *Slouching Towards Bethlehem* (New York: Farrar, Straus & Giroux, 1968), 85.

5. The Beatles, "Happiness is a Warm Gun," Track Eight, Side One, on *The Beatles*, Apple Records, 1968, vinyl LP.

6. Michiko Kakutani, *The New York Times*, "Joan Didion: Staking Out California", June 10, 1979. https://www.nytimes.com/1979/06/10/books/didion-calif.html.

A Wonder Woman in White Tights

By Monica Corcoran Harel

JOAN DIDION'S STYLE ICON status is as much a part of her reputation as her literary canon. What female fan hasn't leaned in closer to squint at photos of her swallowed whole by languid, liquid caftans and wearing those tea saucer-sized sunglasses? Her lit cigarette, almost always held elegantly aloft in the crook of two tapered fingers, smolders like her amused stare. Don't even get me started on that famous shot of her in Hollywood, posing with the hot-shit Corvette. Like the slightly askew center part in her silky chestnut hair, it's all too cool to be uncalculated.

Personally, I prefer my writers paunchy and less photogenic—all that hunching and conjuring transitions takes its toll on the bottom line. Think Shirley Jackson with her uncanny inability to meet the gaze of a camera lens or perpetually rumpled Iris Murdoch, who looks, in most snapshots, like someone has a Bowie knife to her back. But Didion, always sylph-like in photos, makes it look so effortless. Wake up. Part hair a little crooked. Shimmy into maxi dress. Light cigarette. Inhale. Write award-winning prose. Exhale. Did she ever procrastinate by gnawing on a hangnail until her finger throbbed and bloodied her keyboard? Did she ever run to the supermarket with cat hair on her caftan? Did she ever make one single sartorial misstep?

On her now revered "To Pack and Wear" list, which was published in *The White Album* and has since been referenced by every media outlet from *Vogue* to *Vice*, she itemizes "stockings" between a single "bra" and "2 pair shoes."[1] Didion posted this typed packing planner in her Hollywood house to streamline her travel prep as a peripatetic journalist often on assignment. There are no mentions of cut, color, or designers. Call it fashion wrung out to a working uniform.

It's easy to envision Didion gently rinsing out her "stockings" in a motel bathroom sink, massaging the coil of silky nylon with one hand as she smokes with the other. Does she glance up at the mirror pimpled with oxidation and study her face? I think so. I suspect that she practiced the conspiratorial smirk that became her go-to expressions in photographs. In each one, she stares directly into the lens with somewhat stricken eyes and full lips tilted ever so slightly upward.

But it is a black-and-white photo of Didion, taken in April of 1967, that stands out to me. Picture Golden Gate Park on a crisp, cloudy day. The writer had alit in the Bay Area to embed herself with acid droppers, activists, idealists, and drifters that went by names like "Deadeye" and "The Connection." Just three months earlier, more than twenty thousand dewy, disenfranchised youths had converged on the city for a "Human Be-In" that christened the counterculture. The Summer of Love would kick off soon.

Didion was in San Francisco on assignment for the *Saturday Evening Post* to capture the thornier side of the flower power movement. She summed up the resistance as "social hemorrhaging."[2] Her essay not only gilded her career as a literary great but forever hijacked the phrase "slouching towards Bethlehem" from W. B. Yeats, who wrote a variation on it in 1919.

In this picture by photojournalist Ted Streshinsky, Didion is thirty-two but could pass for years younger. But there is no fringed leather poncho or peace sign. In fact, the writer stands by a horde of hippies and looks as buttoned up and parochial as a parson's wife visiting the big city from Ohio. Her jacket might be a Barbour, the sturdy Brit legacy brand favored by outdoorsy, ruddy-faced royals; a huge, knotted silk scarf swaddles her neck. Didion's hair literally bobs below her ear, where she may have dabbed a fingerprint of Givenchy's *L'Interdit* or *L'Air du Temps*.

Didion's style below the waist is equally uncool in this context—and makes her all the more endearing to me. Her dark skirt falls an inch above her knees and could be called a conservative mini. But it's the "stockings" from her packing list that boggle. We're not talking about sheer hosiery with a hint of shimmer or sexy black stockings favored by modern dancers and beatniks in the 1960s. Instead, she wears thick, opaque white tights with flat Mary Janes that appear to be patent leather. While everyone around her turns on, tunes in, and drops out, Didion looks about as psychedelic as a slice of Wonder Bread.

But back to the white tights. I can assure you that these milky, opaque stockings positively stunt the leg line and make your knees look like battered baseballs. After all, they are the hosiery of no-nonsense 1950s nurses and plump four-year-old ballerinas. Even in 1988, when the bitchiest of bitches in the cult film *Heathers* paired white tights with cherry red culottes, the look didn't spur a trend. Every five or so years, fashion editors and designers declare them *de rigueur* and a few women venture out looking like statues with marble legs. But trust me, no one has figured out how to make white tights chic. Not even Didion.

Of her packing list, Didion once said, "Notice the deliberate anonymity of costume: in a skirt, a leotard, and stockings, I could pass on either side of the culture."[3] In this instance in 1967, however, she failed. Just imagine Didion in her prim white tights and shiny party girl shoes on a seedy couch in Haight-Ashbury, watching hippies take tabs of acid. Does she disdainfully cross her legs and glare at a smudge of grime on her snow-white knee? If anything, she may have been mistaken for someone's uptight straight-laced cousin who voted for Barry Goldwater. (Incidentally, she did just that.)

Certainly, this snapshot doesn't portend the glamorous Didion who would go on to curl up in a wicker peacock chair for the camera or pose on a picturesque deck in Malibu. Her smirk back then is softer and less studied too. She looks to me like a writer who might sneeze cracker crumbs onto a computer screen and later mistake one for punctuation. Or the type of woman who would rather nap than pose in front of a muscle car. Most fashionable Didion devotees will opt for the style icon. Me? I prefer her in white tights.

ENDNOTES:

1. Joan Didion, "The White Album," in *The White Album* (New York: Simon & Schuster, 1979), 34.

2. Joan Didion, "Slouching Towards Bethlehem," in *Slouching Towards Bethlehem* (New York: Farrar, Straus & Giroux, 1968), 85.

3. Didion, "The White Album," 35.

No Milk Today:
Revisiting My Haight-Ashbury

By Alysia Abbott

I UNDERSTOOD THE HAIGHT-ASHBURY as home long before I ever knew of it as a place, an idea, or a state of mind. I remember neighborhood potlucks, where I'd fall asleep on a pile of coats; the short walk every day from our apartment to the Haight-Ashbury Day Care Center; playing in Golden Gate Park where the smell of eucalyptus and the nineteenth-century architecture made for the most potent games of pretend. As a child I often dreamt of this park, where playground swings grew twenty feet long and the ponds trilled with insects and frogs.

My father and I moved to the Haight, our first and final neighborhood in San Francisco, in 1974. I was three years old, he thirty. And we were both transplants from Atlanta, Georgia, trying to pick up the pieces of our lives after my mother's fatal car crash the year before. San Francisco was the obvious choice for my dad. He'd come out to my mother before I was born and the city was just starting to emerge as a queer mecca, a place where men and women could be their true selves, in whatever form that entailed. He also had some friends from Atlanta's gay community who'd already settled into the city and helped ease our transition, introducing us to future roommates and showing us how to apply for government assistance.

Seven years had passed between when Didion published "Slouching Towards Bethlehem" in the *Saturday Evening Post* and our own move to the city. Many of the pretty young girls and boys she wrote about had gone home, while the drug dealers who preyed on them remained. Janis Joplin had died. The Grateful Dead had moved on. Most of the groovy storefronts were shut down or boarded up, though others still sold their fabrics and art supplies. The Victorian homes were also in disrepair. I remember dusty peeling exteriors, rooms smelling of cat pee and patchouli, and always feeling a little too cold where I slept (drafts). But these bohemian hovels often revealed the most beautiful gardens round the back, tended to by residents seeking to create their own Eden. Run-down homes meant cheap rent. The neighborhood still attracted waves of people looking to find themselves and a community who would help them on their path—whether that be through Sufi dancing, poetry, cleansing auras, or cosmic sex.

By 1974, the hippie fad and fashions may have been passé, but its legacy was not. Weekends meant puppet shows in the Panhandle and Golden Gate Park. The Cockettes and then the Angels of Light put on free, LSD-fueled performances. And our favorite local restaurant, Mommy Fortuna's, hosted drag acts featuring friends and neighbors. Our Haight-Ashbury was where the free love movement met the gay rights movement, and it was creatively fertile.

But so many of us Gen-Xers were force-fed nostalgia about the Woodstock generation that we became cynical and embittered about the hippie ethos. You can hear this in Nirvana's sarcastically off-key cover of the Byrds' "Come on People," that opens "Territorial Pissings." I think part of the reason Didion's essay was so groundbreaking was because she was one of the first writers to puncture the self-important narrative Baby Boomers had drilled into us. Her reporting and trenchant observation reads with as much urgency today as it did in 1967. "We were seeing the desperate attempt of a handful of pathetically ill-equipped children to create a community in a social vacuum. Once we had seen these children, we could no longer overlook the vacuum, no longer pretend that society's atomization could be reversed."[1]

On reading Didion's essay now I'm struck more by the small children, not the teenagers running away from "bummer" dress codes and curfews, but the children of the men and women setting up homes in the neighborhood—three-year-old Michael, "a very blonde and pale and dirty child on a rocking horse with no paint,"[2] who started a fire, and Susan, the five-year-old in "High Kindergarten,"[3] on acid. I played among these kids in the parks and cluttered apartments. At the Haight-Ashbury Day Care center, we broke macrobiotic bread and snacked on carob stars. As a rule, we were strictly denied white flour and refined sugar but also the security of close supervision by responsible adults. My earliest memories place me alone in our apartment, or left alone while the grown-ups are partying in the other room. I put my finger into a light socket and receive a painful shock that confuses me. In another memory I put my animals to bed under a blanket with a bare-bulb lamp, to shield them from the dark that frightens me. When the blanket starts to burn, a bad smell fills the air. Each of these instances is met with pain and confusion. I know I've made trouble but don't know what I've done wrong.

Whatever bad happened then—the pain, the smell, and the bugs that crawled over unwashed dishes—always felt like my fault, evidence of my essential badness, not the fault of the adults who'd left me alone. That feeling still lives inside my bones. When I'm in an extremely messy space, or involved in a disorganized function, my anxiety rises. I look for "the adult in the room." I was never purposely fed acid or drugs, like Susan. But in his journals, my father writes about dropping acid while watching me at home. One time, when I was four, I'd asked for a bowl of cereal for breakfast. He got out a large salad bowl and poured in the whole box. I immediately burst into tears.

Later, in my teen and early adult years, I felt oppressed by the myth of the Haight-Ashbury, the supposed freedom it promised. Our corner attracted Deadheads, drifters, and runaways that eroded the feasibility of actually living in the neighborhood. Two doors down from the intersection of Haight and Ashbury, I couldn't walk to the store without being hit up for change. Our entranceway was sometimes treated as a public bathroom. I gravitated toward post-punk and new wave and grew to hate the Dead, their followers, and really all that stupid hippie shit.

But maybe the real reason I reviled the hippie movement is because I blamed it for my mother's death. Like I said, my dad came out before I was born, after my parents married. They met in 1968, the same year young French revolutionaries shouted: "Be realistic. Demand the impossible." So, they demanded the impossible: a healthy open marriage fueled by psychedelics. Though married, Dad took lovers on the side and so did my mom, including a young guy who got arrested running drugs. On the way back from bailing that kid out of jail, my mom's car was rear-ended, an accident which ended her life on a foggy street in Sweetwater, Tennessee. I couldn't help but resent the irresponsibility of this generation, throwing youth, beauty, and intelligence into the fire, like sacrificial lambs. In some ways I feel like my mom was a casualty of the sexual revolution.

I don't know if my dad ever considered the weight of this history on me, or even owned the impact of his loose parenting style. He still believed I could weather whatever scenario I found myself in better than the pain of growing up as he did, in a repressed middle-class home in 1950s Nebraska, where he was spanked for the audacity of running naked onto the lawn. Dad felt he couldn't trust anyone with his inner life then, so he made a point of sharing his with me, and taking an interest in mine. For all the times I was left on my own, or he was late to pick me up from school, or our place was a mess, or he didn't notice me dating way older guys, I never, not for one moment, doubted his love.

◆◆◆

IN HER INTRODUCTION TO *Slouching Towards Bethlehem*, Didion wrote that her Haight-Ashbury piece was the most imperative of the collection's essays, but also the least understood. "I have never gotten feedback so universally beside the point," she wrote. The essay, she argues, wasn't just about "a handful of children wearing mandalas on their foreheads," or the isolated "filth"[4] of the Haight-Ashbury, but a more general malaise, a sense that the culture was eating itself. "All that seemed clear was at some point we had aborted ourselves and butchered the job."[5]

Didion was one of the few journalists of her day who saw through the romance of the movement, the Haight-Ashbury captured in the photographs of Herb Greene and in the Top 40 songs that have known eternal life via classic rock radio and Sirius XM. She shines a sharp light on its darker corners: the runaways, the raped, the drug-addled kids. The Haight-Ashbury she describes is a utopian ideal gone horribly wrong, evidence that without guardians, without guardrails, unchecked idealism results in dangerous self-harm, a generation that was destroying itself. The idea of a child being fed LSD is as horrifying in 2019 as it was in 1967, but reading it, I feel that she seizes on this detail to make a point about the waste of youth, the future. She shares the lyrics to the Herman's Hermits song she repeatedly hears on the radio while reporting: "No Milk Today."

That said, I wonder what Joan would think of today's Haight-Ashbury.

The Haight and other neighborhoods have been cleaned up, infused with vast amounts of money coming from the tech revolution. The one-bedroom I shared with my dad rented for $425 a month just before I moved out in 1994. The average one-bedroom in the city now rents for $3,600. Today's Haight-Ashbury is a Disney ride version of itself, with expensive head shops and high-end boutiques and murals depicting the long-gone icons. The San Francisco that's emerged from the dot-com boom, and the growth of local companies Twitter, Google, and Airbnb, has been as full of "brave hopes and national promise"[6] as the San Francisco of 1967. The city still attracts young people eager to transform culture but now they call it "disruption," and they seek to disrupt through business and technology. Instead of dropping acid they micro-dose. The new San Franciscans may no longer be physically endangered but they are spiritually endangered. I'm not the only one to fear that capitalism unchecked is poisoning the social well. As in 1967, "a great many articulate people seem to have a sense of high social purpose,"[7] but today that purpose is driven by capital, a far cry from what all those silly hippies were after.

Vestiges of the San Francisco we loved are closing every day. Few of the city's original gay bars remain. The quirky restaurants and cafés that used to host poetry readings and shows have also closed. Cafés can't retain staff, even with a fifteen-dollar minimum hourly wage. Who can live on fifteen dollars an hour in a city transformed by innovation? Of all the people I knew growing up and working in the city, only a tiny handful remain. Many, like my dad, died of AIDS. Others have been Ellis-acted out of rent-controlled apartments, or driven out of the city by high rent and low job prospects, or just left because they didn't feel welcome anymore. My childhood best friend, a third-generation San Franciscan whose black family owned a sports store in the Haight for twenty-three years, drove an Uber to supplement her retail work before finally moving in with a cousin in Nashville. She reports the southern city is both more diverse and friendlier to people of color. Can you imagine saying that in 1967?

The promise of San Francisco lived on long past that Summer of Love. The city, for all its quirks and faults, was gloriously both an anomaly and a refuge. Now it is neither.

I still dream of the Haight, especially the one-bedroom apartment I shared with my dad for thirteen years. There, I find fabulous hidden rooms—how did I not know this was here?— or boxes of clothes and notebooks I didn't know I'd left behind. I walk through Buena Vista Park and try to take in as much of the neighborhood as I can before rushing myself back to the airport. I'm always late for my flight. There's never enough time.

ENDNOTES:

1. Joan Didion, "Slouching Towards Bethlehem," in *Slouching Towards Bethlehem* (New York: Farrar, Straus and Giroux, 1968), 122-23.
2. Didion, "Slouching Towards Bethlehem," 95.
3. Didion, "Slouching Towards Bethlehem," 127.
4. Joan Didion, "A Preface," in *Slouching Towards Bethlehem* (New York: Farrar, Straus and Giroux, 1968), xii.
5. Didion, "Slouching Towards Bethlehem," 85.
6. Didion, "Slouching Towards Bethlehem," 85.
7. Didion, "Slouching Towards Bethlehem," 84.

Brentwood Notebook

By Stacie Stukin

1.

BRENTWOOD, LIKE MUCH OF the best real estate in California, was once a Rancho. In the 1830s, these lands with their adobe houses and cattle ranches were bestowed upon landed gentry called Californios, descended from or married into families of Spanish-speaking settlers from Mexico and Spain who came to the Golden State a century earlier. The Ranchos stretched from the oceans to the mountains and many were originally home to the Gabrielino Tongva tribe, whom the Catholic Church enslaved to build their missions and forced to hear their sermons.

I grew up in what was once the Rancho San Vicente y Santa Monica, a 33,000-acre parcel that included Santa Monica, Brentwood, Mandeville Canyon, and West Los Angeles. The Tongva called this area Kuruvunga, which translates as *A Place Where We Are in the Sun*, but in the 1870s when the Californios began selling off their land grants, all that was left of the village were pottery shards and grinding stones that the earth spit out when real estate investors dug into the ground to develop the rustic canyons, mesas, and foothills verdant with oaks, sycamores, grasses, and game like coyote, snake, rabbit, and birds.

Even the roads harkened back to the Tongva; their footpath ran through the Sepulveda basin from the city into the San Fernando Valley. Eventually, in the 1920s it was paved, and during the following decades, demand for more roadway ushered in the earthmovers. In the 1960s, they tore through the mountains and gouged an 1,800-foot-wide and 260-foot-deep passage, accomplishing in twenty-four months what should have taken millions of years if left to natural erosion. Thus, the 405 Freeway was born to transport us and, ultimately, torment us with traffic.

I tell you all this not as a history lesson but to give you context, a sense of where I come from and how this destruction, creation, and neighborhood building was my land too. I played with the other children in the gullies and streams that ran behind our house way up in the hills of Mandeville Canyon. I could wake up on late spring mornings and a heavy layer of marine fog hovered in the air, creating a voile-like curtain through which I could see a family of deer grazing on our lawn. On hot summer nights, as I slept surrounded by furniture my father built in my antique twin brass bed covered in a blue Pierre Deux coverlet, I would awaken to the high-pitched, frenzied shrieks of coyotes, who stalked neighborhood pets. In the morning, I might hear news of a cat that had gone missing, or even more grisly, someone down the block might discover the shredded remains of a small fluffy dog who could not outrun the pack.

In the 1970s and 1980s, the neighborhood still felt as it was described in a 1907 *Los Angeles Times* advertisement that touted Brentwood as "a suburb away from the noise, dust and inharmonies of the city," and encouraged prospective residents not to miss an opportunity to live among "people of refinement" who "love

Brentwood Park for its breadth of view—its variety of scene—its everlasting breezes—its naturalness." It was, and still is, an affluent neighborhood but back then, even with Los Angeles's debilitating smog, there was reasonably priced housing stock—newly built post and beam houses suited both in price and style to young couples like my parents. Some said it was the closest facsimile of waspy Connecticut in Southern California. Women drove wood-paneled station wagons or Volvos, and there were country clubs and beach clubs that didn't allow Jewish families like mine (of course, there were tokens). The older homes —from the 1930s housing boom—were built in traditional styles like Spanish Colonial Revival, Georgian Revival, or Tudor and attracted celebrities like Marilyn Monroe, Joan Crawford, and Gregory Peck. During my era Dustin Hoffman, Joan Didion, John Gregory Dunne, and O. J. Simpson were some of the more notable residents. It was a friendly suburb. You knew your neighbors. You saw them at the grocery store, at the candy store, and at the local pizza place.

Back then, if someone asked me where I lived, they'd often say, "Where's Brentwood?" I'd explain it was between Westwood and Santa Monica, north of San Vicente Boulevard where the coral trees with their blood red blooms and their craggy, bent limbs line the thoroughfare.

It was a time of hands-off parenting, a feral youth with hard edges that offered an independence, a lack of supervision that had us stumbling into trouble without our parents ever being privy to the twisted plots. The dramas were tempered by a climate where gardenias flourished, only to be plucked off bushes and put in small vases bedside. The waft of the exotic scent accompanied our dreams and the jasmine that blossomed from spring through summer, with its sweet, musky aroma, seemed an apt metaphor for our temptations and longings.

2.

"MEET AT THE TOP of Capri." It was a vague direction but we knew where to go since some of the neighborhood boys, scions of Dohenys, had taken us there. They blasted Pink Floyd and Led Zeppelin from the Alpine stereo so we could hear the guitar riffs over the rev of the engine in their Shelby Mustang. They must have figured out the Ronald Reagan house was empty, as the family had put it up for sale when they moved to Washington to become the fortieth First Family.

At the time, I didn't realize the Reagan house, built in 1957 on a bluff high in the Santa Monica mountains, had been called the "the house of the future." It wasn't the traditional home you'd imagine that the Reagans might occupy. Instead, the spiffy midcentury modern, 5,000-square-foot ranch-style home, with its sweeping vista from city to sea, satisfied the actors' desire for a view and an octagon-shaped pool. When it was built, Reagan hosted the General Electric Theater, a weekly CBS science series that reached twenty-five million viewers, making it one of the most popular shows on TV, and General Electric had outfitted the home with every kind of electrical innovation.

The house was part of GE's "Live Better Electrically" marketing campaign, and on several episodes the Reagans hosted the show at home, demonstrating the energy-saving devices that controlled the temperature, heat, and light. Nancy Reagan spoke highly of the "electric servants" in her kitchen that she said, "make mommy's work easier": perfect melted-cheese toast, the best coffee Ronnie ever tasted, and ovens with timers and temperature controls that prevented her soufflés from exploding.

As Nancy grinded the residue of her soufflé dinners down the garbage disposal and marveled how the dining room chandelier with color controls looked "like a necklace of jewels," Reagan traveled the country as a GE spokesperson, giving him the national exposure that not only boosted his political career but helped convince him to change his party affiliation from Democrat to Republican. His message was one of deregulation and advocacy for free enterprise, a stance that landed him in the California statehouse and then in the White House.

When Reagan was elected president in 1981, I was a junior in high school and didn't care about and could not anticipate his impact. I had no inkling that during college I would be riveted by the televised Iran-Contra congressional hearings of National Security Council aide Oliver North, who facilitated a scheme where profits of secret weapon sales to Iran were diverted to arm the anti-Sandinista Contras in Nicaragua—a tale of gun running and drug trafficking that seemed more movie plot than political reality. I did not yet know the impact of HIV on my friends and a whole generation of talented men who would be lost to us. I couldn't imagine that Reagan would never say the word AIDS until 1987, let alone fund any significant research. And I could not anticipate that Nancy Reagan, who had become known for her red dresses and a predilection for astrologers, would proffer ironic glee with her preposterous "Just Say No" anti-drug campaign in 1986. After all, the road to the Reagans' home was where we went to party.

We'd drive down Sunset Boulevard, then turn north up Capri until we hit a dark dirt road. We were drunk or high on weed, or both. Sometimes cocaine was involved or Quaaludes—the latter didn't appeal to me, just made my legs wobble and didn't offer the consciousness shift I craved: an urge to feel something different than the confines of convention, a comforting obliteration. One particular night, I drove up the dark windy road with a girlfriend.

We arrived at the fire road adjacent to the house, which was just a shadow in the distance. We parked the car on the plateau that opened to a wide expanse. We were on top of our world. The city lights below, the stars above, and the cool air, but not so cold that we needed jackets over our jumpsuits in some shade of neon, and lips most likely adorned with Revlon Cherries in the Snow. We opened the sunroof, left the car doors open, and cranked the volume of a cassette mixtape. The B-52s, "Planet Claire." Our alienated anthem. The Pretenders, "Precious." We yelled *Fuck-off!* into the night.

3.

ON AUGUST 19, 1970, prosecutors in the Tate murder trial called Timothy Ireland to the stand. He was the first witness after former Manson follower Linda Kasabian, who cooperated with the prosecution, and concluded eighteen days of testimony. During the trial, Kasabian wore at least one dress purchased for her by Joan Didion at I. Magnin in Beverly Hills. The writer developed a relationship with the Manson follower after visiting her at the Sybil Brand Institute for women while reporting on the brutal murders. On this Wednesday, Kasabian wore her hair in pigtails, and a long-sleeved orange dress and moccasins.

Ireland was the afternoon witness. A graduate student employed by the Westlake School for Girls, Ireland was hired to supervise a "sleep-out" on the campus tucked in the wealthy residential enclave of Holmby Hills. In the early morning hours of August 9, 1969 he heard something. According to the police report, "Between 0100 and 0130 Mr. Ireland was awake, alert and watching the sleeping children. He heard a male voice from what seemed to him a long distance away to the north or northeast shout, 'Oh, God, no. Stop. Stop. Oh, God, no, don't.' Ireland said that the scream persisted for approximately ten seconds. The male voice was clear and he did not notice an accent." During the trial, Ireland said he got in his car to search for the source of the screams and found nothing. When cross-examined by Manson's lawyer who asked him if he documented what he heard, he replied, "No sir. You don't forget things like that."[1]

I attended the Westlake School for Girls from 1976–1982. I discovered the Manson connection when I read my parents' paperback copy of the book *Helter Skelter* by the prosecutor Vincent Bugliosi and Curt Gentry. I quickly found Ireland's story on page four, a scene setter with the ominous proviso: "The canyons above Hollywood and Beverly Hills play tricks with sounds. A noise clearly audible a mile away may be indistinguishable at a few hundred feet."[2] The site of the murder on Cielo Drive was about a mile from the bucolic campus. From the center of campus, if you looked up toward the hills to the North, you could see the homes lining the ridge of Benedict Canyon near Sharon Tate and Roman Polanski's house.

The Spanish Colonial Revival campus built in the 1920s by architects Arthur Kelly and Joe Estep—the same men who designed the nearby Playboy Mansion—was a single-sex education Shangri-La with rolling lawns, flowers, and a Maypole that was paraded out every spring so we could dance around the phallus and weave colorful ribbon patterns as we celebrated the pagan rite of spring. We wore uniforms—gray skirts, white oxford long-sleeved shirts, and navy-and-white saddle shoes with pink, eraser-colored soles. My classmates included the daughters of influential Los Angelenos like Tom Snyder (the talk show host who famously interviewed Manson in 1981), philanthropists, and real estate magnates like Helen and Peter Bing, the daughters of Carole Burnett and Peter Fonda, and Joan Didion and John Gregory Dunne's daughter, Quintana.

The Los Angeles of my high school years was the LA of *American Gigolo*, with muted pastel interiors inside buildings that retained the character of a city built with a panoply of styles, where you could get anywhere in twenty minutes by car. Yet, percolating beneath Richard Gere's sleek Armani wardrobe and the glamour of Lauren Hutton's trench coat and her burgundy Bottega Veneta clutch, there was an underlying darkness, a roughness. It seemed all was not well. We were a generation of divorce. Some of us were neglected or had parents who were alcoholic or whose alcohol we drank. During the week we did our homework, sometimes up to three hours a night. And despite the English teacher who failed me on every paper I wrote, I persisted. I scribbled observations in journals, on scraps of paper, in frantic letters to friends and boyfriends.

Although I was burdened by a feeling of never quite connecting, being an outsider who preferred detachment to real engagement did not mean I wasn't inspired by my privileged education. At the time, I did not understand the nature of that privilege or how, later in life, it would impact how others viewed me. Back then, we slogged through Jane Austen's *Northanger Abbey*, read Thomas Hardy's *Tess of the d'Urbervilles*, replete with Maypole dancing, and when we discussed Kafka's *The Hunger Artist*, I was moved by the idea that one could be so compelled to create that dying for art was a reasonable option. There was the proudly feminist English teacher, who taught us about the ERA and that women made seventy cents to every dollar men earned, and when she assigned Tennessee Williams's *A Streetcar Named Desire*, she read aloud the part of Stanley Kowalski, lumbering across the classroom as she bellowed his lines in order to teach us the difference between consent and rape. We read the poems of Adrienne Rich and Emily Dickinson and learned that a woman's voice is something to be valued even when society might not agree.

But such academic conceits were not always so simple. We had a whisper network. We knew which adults really wanted to hear us and help us develop our voices. And we knew who did not, like the teacher who continuously failed me. Was she angry at my privilege? Did she sense my predilection toward masochism? I perceived this as my hill to climb, to prove that all I wanted was to be a writer and all she wanted to do was tear that dream from me.

I write this not to perpetuate a grudge. I'm more interested in the determination it ignited, the weakness and strength I explored, and the will I developed to push back against obstacles that were not mine alone. I took solace in knowing I was not her only victim. Once, Quintana Dunne turned in an assignment only to have the teacher insist that her mother, Joan Didion, had written the paper. Word traveled. Phone calls were made. Parent-teacher conferences commenced. We knew the teacher picked targets to belittle, and we speculated she just wanted an opportunity to engage with Didion since we had heard her praise the slight woman, wearing dark sunglasses and a camel coat, that we sometimes saw on campus.

We read *The White Album* because we were obsessed with Jim Morrison and titillated by Didion's repeated reference to Morrison's black vinyl pants, worn without underwear. Like The Doors, we took acid to open our doors of perception. We read William Blake and Aldous Huxley, too. That was our privilege. To read poetry, trip on LSD, and wander the Sunset Strip, past the Whiskey-a-Go-Go with the soundtrack of *L.A. Woman* in our heads as we made our way down toward Santa Monica Boulevard to Duke's Coffee Shop in the Tropicana Motel, the very place where Morrison had hung out. And like the children we were, we sat at the counter and ordered cinnamon toast.

We were self-assured teenagers, perhaps entitled, but we had our own sense of justice. We knew the teacher was wrong. We believed Quintana. We understood this was her burden, to be the child of two famous writers. We had our own burdens so we had faith in each other. We had to. We were raising ourselves and each other, forging a path toward adulthood. We had things to say. And our privileged education had taught us that our ideas mattered, that our voices should be heard.

4.

AT 12:10 A.M. ON June 13, 1994, Nicole Brown and Ron Goldman were found murdered in Brentwood. The bodies were slashed, the scene was bloody, and it seemed the only witness was Nicole's dog Kato, an Akita who was found howling as he roamed the neighborhood with bloody paws. If only the dog could talk, they said.

At the time of the murders, I had long since moved out of my parents' house and any evidence of the nostalgia of my childhood had disappeared. It was excavated out of existence when the local grocery store became a Whole Foods and when the scene of the crime on Bundy Drive became a tourist attraction.

I rarely return to Brentwood. My parents have passed away and it is now home to Gwyneth and Reese, and while that level of fame always existed, it was not a flashy time rife with paparazzi, or selfie desperation. Teslas with winged doors and $150,000 Mercedes G-Wagons with tinted windows did not hog the road or cut you off with bold lane changes.

The iconic coral trees are dying. There is a campaign to save them. They are old and have fallen victim to borers—insect eggs that hatch into larvae, burrow deep into the branches and kill them. The residential streets, once lined with majestic front yards giving view to the traditional architecture, are now walls of security gates and tall hedges to prevent gawkers from seeing McMansions in the form of steroidal Cape Cods or modern boxes that look more like hotels than homes.

The house that Joan Didion and John Gregory Dunne lived in with Quintana was torn down soon after they sold it, in 1988. In *The Year of Magical Thinking*, Didion describes driving by the property and discovering only a chimney standing on an empty lot. She recalls how the real estate agent had asked her and Dunne to inscribe copies of the books they'd written in the house, because it would be meaningful to the buyers. "When we saw the flattened lot from the car, Quintana, in the back seat, burst into tears," she writes. "My first reaction was fury. I wanted the books back."[3]

My childhood home still stands. I can see it on Google maps, pixelated but still recognizable. Ronald Reagan's house was torn down to make way for a Spanish-style manse; O. J. Simpson's house was demolished, too. But in what was once the heart of the Tongva village, Kuruvunga, a natural hot spring surrounded by native plants still flows. It's one of the tribe's last remaining historical landmarks, a sacred site, a place where we are all in the sun.

Endnotes:

1. "Tate First Homicide Investigation Progress Report," http://www.mansondirect.com/police-report-tate-1st.html
2. Vincent Bugliosi and Curt Gentry, *Helter Skelter: The True Story of the Manson Murders* (W.W. Norton & Co., 1974), 4.
3. Joan Didion, *The Year of Magical Thinking* (Alfred A. Knopf, 2005), 133–34.

On Keeping a Cookbook

By Heather John Fogarty

"What is a recipe for sauerkraut doing in my notebook?"[1] Joan Didion asks in her essay "On Keeping a Notebook," first published in the December 1966 issue of *Holiday*. For Didion, the act of keeping a notebook is less a means of factually recording an event, than of experiencing how the moment felt. The notebook becomes an active examination of the self. The same might be said of writing down her recipes.

When I first heard rumblings about a Didion documentary back in 2014, I hurried over to the Kickstarter campaign to pledge at a level that would land me a PDF of *Joan's Recipe Book*—a book that the producers said "represents a lifetime of entertaining." The reward was not limited to a tasteful compendium of recipes (because what else would a recipe book from Joan Didion look like?), but a glimpse into a literary life that centers around writing and food.

You can learn a lot about a person by cooking her recipes. Like Didion's prose, her recipes are often austere and rely on instinct; so much knowledge is assumed. A risotto recipe is laid out in a taut forty-two words. A more lavish presentation for Lamb Navarin (a French stew, to be served outside, she notes) is noncommittal in its quantities for wine and broth. She is similarly evasive in her preparation of *Daube de Boeuf*. While making her *albondigas*, which are essentially Mexican meatballs, I wondered if the size of eggs hadn't increased dramatically since she recorded the recipe as my mix was overly wet, requiring that I add more rice to bind the meatballs. A recipe for crème caramel directs the cook to caramelize sugar and scald milk—at what temperature and for what length of time it does not reveal—with vanilla bean, a sophisticated departure from the standard vanilla extract favored by home cooks.

Some of the recipes in the collection are handwritten on scraps of paper or *LIFE* letterhead; others along with menus and guest lists (heavy on writers, artists, and industry types) are typed on food-stained notecards and loose sheets of paper. Many are annotated copies from magazines and cookbooks. What do the recipes and menus tell us? We know that guests such as Patti Smith ate Lillian Hellman's chicken hash with roasted yellow peppers and arugula vinaigrette, Joseph Lelyveld a produce-heavy spread of cherry tomatoes, avocados, and corn with tarragon and a coleslaw recipe from chef Alice Waters spiked with jalapeños. At an intimate dinner with Christopher Dickey, she serves alongside olives and assorted French goat cheeses some chopped chiles and those albondigas, a dish that garners a first mention in the *Los Angeles Times* in 1895, described as "genuinely native Californian."[2]

So, too, is Didion in her approach to cooking and entertaining, borrowing from Mexican, French, Italian, and Asian influences with locally sourced seasonal produce—or a style of cooking pioneered by the likes of Waters that came to be known in the

1970s as "California cuisine." Didion's evenings generally end with clementines, fresh cherries, plums, and chocolates, depending on what's in season. The recipe book has all the markings of Los Angeles food culture, beyond the ubiquitous avocado and twelve-month growing season. Rather, hers is a seemingly effortless ability to blend cultures and cuisines, and to tell a story by setting the scene. Or in this case, setting the California table.

Joan's Recipe Book might have been the first signal to a wider audience of her love of cooking, but to a closer reader, the evidence has always been on the page. In *The White Album*, Didion recalls "taking a 25-mg. Compazine one Easter Sunday and making a large and elaborate lunch for a number of people, many of whom were still around on Monday."[3] There was the publication of her Mexican Chicken in *The Great American Writers' Cookbook*, a recipe later included in Nora Ephron's self-published cookbook as "Joan Didion's Mexican Chicken Thing," which Ephron amends to include the wearing of medical gloves to protect fingers while chopping chiles, a technique that most certainly distinguishes the Native Californian from the Native New Yorker. (Ephron adds, "Very Lady Macbeth, I think.") Didion, in turn, includes Ephron's recipe for sorrel soup from *Heartburn* in her recipe collection. In several interviews with *The New York Times* her cooking prowess is also mentioned.

But it's in the pages of Didion's own writing where memory and that aforementioned crème caramel with the vanilla beans, for example, represents a summer in the 1970s in which Didion, Katharine Ross and Conrad Hall, and Jean and Brian Moore talked of opening a restaurant together, what she calls a "Malibu survivalist plan" that would have Katherine, Jean, and Joan taking turns cooking while their spouses ran the front of the house. The plan fell apart when Ross and Hall separated, and Moore began work on a new novel.

"I remember that we all made soufflés," Didion writes of this time in *The Year of Magical Thinking*. "Conrad's sister Nancy in Papeete had shown Katherine how to make them work without effort and Katherine showed me and Jean. The trick was a less strict approach than generally advised. Katherine also brought back Tahitian vanilla beans for us, thick sheaves tied with raffia. We did crème caramel with the vanilla for a while but nobody liked to caramelize the sugar."[4]

Around that time, *Vogue* magazine photographed the Didion-Dunnes at their home in Malibu. An outtake from the shoot features the now iconic photograph of Didion in pigtails making stew in her flame-orange Le Creuset against a pink midcentury ceramic-tile backdrop. Images that made the final cut in the October 1972 issue of the magazine include a kitchen detail of French wire *saladière* baskets holding onions, avocados, tomatoes, and garlic that hang above Mexican terra-cotta pots planted with fresh herbs and a Tiffany-blue box filled with handwritten recipe cards. Another shows Didion, Dunne, and their six-year-old daughter Quintana Roo sitting down to a lunch of *Daube de Boeuf* with spring onions and cherry tomatoes, a bottle of French white at the ready. Their lives, the Didion-Dunnes tell the interviewer, revolve around writing, reading, and food. "I learned to cook when I was working as a writer at *Vogue*," Didion says, "as I had to proofread all the recipes. Now both John and I read cookbooks steadily. I love to make stews or soups…When you are writing, you can't know the day before if you want guests. We do have neighbor writer friends that we can call the same day. I think a great soup or stew makes guests go home feeling more attractive than when they came."[5]

The stews recorded in *Joan's Recipe Book* that nourished countless intellectuals overlooking the Pacific at the Didion-

Dunne homes in Portuguese Bend and Malibu, and in town in Hollywood and Brentwood, amount to more than mere instructions for cooking food. Just as the olives, avocados, citrus, and stone fruit that appear throughout her menus and grow on trees in her backyards are more than a snapshot of a California lifestyle, these recipe pages also represent sensory foundations for future and past narratives. In *The Year of Magical Thinking*, Didion recalls the peacocks that nested in the olive trees on their Portuguese Bend property, screaming at dusk and dawn. "One dawn I awoke to the screaming and looked for John," she writes. "I found him outside in the dark, tearing unripe peaches from a tree and hurling them at the peacocks, a characteristically straightforward if counterproductive approach to resolving an annoyance."[6] As she romanticizes the sun porches, avocado trees, and an overgrown clay tennis court in Hollywood, she recalls a framed verse that Earl McGrath had written for her fifth wedding anniversary that concludes with "Living in a style best called erstwhile / On Franklin Avenue."[7] You can imagine the rambling lunches for sixty on Spode china.

Yet a decade later in a 1979 interview in *The New York Times*, Didion describes the dread created by those avocados so often served at spring lunches and on summer nights, this time at her Brentwood Park home. "The exterminator took one look at the backyard and said we were sure to have rats in the avocado tree," Didion says. "That's when I started thinking about bubonic plague."[8]

Why *was* there a recipe for sauerkraut in her notebook? For the same reason she records who came to dinner and what they ate—to create a sense of order and connection to time and place. Just as the recipe book offers subtle insights not only to the type of cook and entertainer she is, it hints at a state of mind that these ingredients evoke. There is safety to be found in nostalgia, even if that safety is imagined and memory parts ways with the reality of the moment. "It all comes back," she writes, one imagines on her Royal KMG at her desk high above the Pacific in Portuguese Bend. "Even that recipe for sauerkraut: even that brings it back. I was on Fire Island when I first made that sauerkraut, and it was raining, and we drank a lot of bourbon and ate the sauerkraut and went to bed at ten, and I listened to the rain and the Atlantic and felt safe. I made the sauerkraut again last night and it did not make me feel any safer, but that is, as they say, another story."[9]

ENDNOTES:

1. Joan Didion, "On Keeping a Notebook," in *Slouching Towards Bethlehem* (New York: Farrar, Straus and Giroux, 1968), 138.
2. "Un Baile Español," in the *Los Angeles Times,* July 7, 1895, 7.
3. Joan Didion, "The White Album," in *The White Album* (New York: Simon & Schuster, 1979), 20.
4. Joan Didion, *The Year of Magical Thinking* (New York: Alfred A. Knopf, 2005), 72-73.
5. "Writers' Roost," *Vogue,* October, 1972.
6. Didion, *The Year of Magical Thinking,* 119.
7. Didion, *The Year of Magical Thinking,* 74.
8. Michiko Kakutani, "Joan Didion: Staking Out California," *The New York Times,* June 10, 1979. https://www.nytimes.com/1979/06/10/books/didion-calif.html
9. Didion, "On Keeping a Notebook," 141.

Red Flag Days:
Living in Joan Didion's Malibu

By Marc Weingarten

WHEN THE WOOLSEY FIRE came to Malibu, the fire that everyone feared would someday come to pass, I was already gone. It was fortuitous in the extreme. I felt like I had dodged a bullet.

Most beachside communities pull you into their hazy lassitude. Taking in the crosswinds and the shimmering horizon, you can feel your pulse slowing down. Malibu doesn't work that way. Paradise here doesn't mean keeping things simple; it means making a compact with a landscape that will always bite back. To live in Malibu, you have to hold two ideas simultaneously in your brain: things can't get any better, but at any time they could get a lot worse.

Joan Didion, who regarded postwar California as a grand social experiment that leaked out too many casualties, was drawn to Malibu for its remoteness as much as its beauty. Didion's home in 1971 was far north in Trancas Canyon, a short drive from the Ventura border and a world removed from the "Beverly Hills on the Beach" enclaves in southern Malibu.

For thirteen years I lived two miles south of Trancas, in a remote cul-de-sac tucked behind the city's only public high school. The idea was: breathing room, clean air, healthy life, quiet writing time. But I felt marooned, thrown off my axis. Malibu itself is geographically off-putting—a city bisected by a busy highway. There is nothing quaint or charming here, no historic Main Street for tourists to stroll. Unlike every other iconic beach community, Malibu is notable for what it lacks. As Didion observed in "Quiet Days in Malibu," from *The White Album*, it has "no passable restaurant, nothing to attract the traveler's dollar."[1] Things have changed a bit since she jotted down those impressions, but not much: it's just three outdoor malls ringed by parking lots, the mountains to the east, the ocean to the west. If you don't embrace this fact, you will be miserable there.

When I first arrived, I brought along the myths I'd gleaned from Ray Chandler and Robert Altman, Gidget and Brian Wilson, marveling at its beauty while trying to look beyond the glassy sheen into its authentic soul. But Malibu doesn't give up its secrets so easily; people move here to shunt themselves off. In short, it's good for novelists and bad for journalists. Trying to really uncover anything interesting in a place like this is as tough an assignment as sussing out black truffles in the Dordogne.

Joan Didion didn't come to Malibu expecting to find stories, but she found them anyway. Mostly, she was drawn to Malibu's natural environment after living in a grand old Hollywood house for seven years with her husband John Gregory Dunne and their daughter, Quintana Roo. Didion took to the provincialism of the place: "We exchanged information at the Trancas Market," she wrote in "Quiet Days." "We left packages and messages for one another at the Gulf Station...A rattlesnake in my driveway meant its mate in yours."[2]

To understand Malibu through the prism of Didion's thought, you don't have to go to the essay she specifically wrote about it. It's also there in "The Seacoast of Despair," from *Slouching Towards Bethlehem*, her piece about Newport, Rhode Island and its Gilded Age palaces, built by men whose enormous wealth fostered an "entrapment in the mechanics of living";[3] or her meditation on Hawaiian culture, "Letter from Paradise, 21' 19' N., 157' 52' W," also from *Slouching*, with its "boys in search of the perfect wave" and "children who have never been told…that golden lads and girls all must as chimney sweepers come to dust."[4]

The barons are walled in by the appurtenances of their material wealth; the surfer dudes hold proprietary claims on waves. Yet none of them can stake a claim to the land. So it is in Malibu, a region in flux, frangible and prone to great and frequent irruptions of environmental disorder.

◆◆◆

SEVEN THINGS THAT HAPPENED to me in Malibu:

From my bedroom window, I watched a coyote snatch my daughter's terrier in its jaws and scoot down the hill. I chased it in my underwear until it jumped a nine-foot fence, the dog still in its mouth.

Another view from my bedroom: A blue-ochre flash of fire burning in a canyon south of us. It looked close, but it wasn't. When I turned around, my wife had already awakened the kids in a panic and driven off. She was still barefoot. The next day, I went to work.

On the day before we moved out, a brush fire erupted, and this time it was close—just a few feet from our house. Water-bearing helicopters raked across the sky so low you could read the serial numbers on their bellies.

I commuted two hours to work for ten years.

At Zuma Beach, three dolphins swam so close to shore that I wanted to jump in with them. Turned out they were an advance team for two whales, who breached so high and so regally that it made our mouths drop.

I made new friends, and I lost some old ones.

I spotted a bobcat on the Backbone trail. It looked at us with disdain; I swear he sneered at us. We went our separate ways, and I never saw another bobcat again.

◆◆◆

"QUIET DAYS IN MALIBU" was written in pieces from 1976 to 1978, a time when the community was a cow town of sorts, at least on the north side. Since then, it has become something else—overdeveloped, overexposed, clogged with thousands of inlanders on summer weekends. Yet it still retains much of the character of its backwater past; strict zoning laws prevent the city from becoming choked with Sunglass Huts and Wetzel's Pretzels. So, even though Lady Gaga dropped $23 million on a house across the highway from Zuma, it feels apart.

But nature here gives and takes away. Driving north on PCH, you can spot the signposts of disaster averted: metal mesh nets that resemble Christo installations holding back the crumbly hillside; signs that gauge daily fire danger; old burn areas that erratically bloom on the major mountain passes. There is an active fault system that runs the length of the Santa Monica Mountains that cradle the city; there are fault lines in the ocean, as well. These are the things that tourists overlook and locals regard as battle scars. To live in Malibu is to live with visual reminders of one's own provisional relationship to it.

As a subject for literary inquiry, Malibu has virtually no lineage to speak of. Joan Didion owns the territory. She arrived wanting to swim with the seals and raise her family in a sane environment, only to discover a place where Manifest Destiny crashed against the shoals of a capricious landscape. In her Malibu essay, she presents us with a community that is held together by "shared isolation and adversity," where a 69,000-acre brush fire in nearby Canejo Valley sends great gunmetal clouds of smoke over the Santa Monica Mountains, at which point Malibu becomes most "perilously and breathtakingly itself."[5] This is Mike Davis's "Sunshine and Noir" dialectic in its starkest form: A region of astonishing beauty whose portents come and go as they please.

Didion enjoyed her isolation in Malibu; it was suitable to her melancholy temperament. So it is for the city's old-timers, who find themselves caged in their homes when the summer hordes clog up Pacific Coast Highway. Or, as in the case of the Woolsey Fire in November 2018, they are socked in by a raging blaze and unable to escape in any direction lest they melt in their cars. Part of a community's strength is drawn from its ability to endure something difficult together, and Malibu's history is defined by such moments. In an era of fractiousness and atomization, Didion found comfort in that fact. Didion intuited this hunkering down as part of your civic duty here, of keeping out of the way and enjoying your isolation as a gift rather than a burden. "I never loved the house of Pacific Coast Highway more than when it was impossible to leave it,"[6] she wrote.

I felt otherwise: that feeling of being imprisoned in such moments, of not having the agency of mobility, felt antithetical to the spirit of the place. Didion knew that this was precisely why Malibu stood apart. It didn't open itself up to you like a dream from a picture postcard. Paradise is not handed or owed to you here. It's earned.

Throughout "Quiet Days," Didion offers ominous murmurings: Writing on Thanksgiving Day from her deck, she sees a plume of smoke from a fire stretching out over the ocean. She is insisting that there is nothing out of the ordinary here. It's just a Malibu day in November, and that smoke is as intrinsic as whitecaps and Hobies strapped to Chevy wagons.

When in Malibu, one must accept that nature will always have its way; it is annealed into the life of the community. And so one must go about one's business. One day Didion visits Amado Vasquez, a "resident alien" who grows orchids in a greenhouse owned by Hollywood producer Arthur Freed. Didion admires Vasquez's hedgehog-like commitment to growing plants that are among the most intransigent to cultivate, in an artificial environment that feels to her like a *Sanctum Santorum*, a reliquary of nature's beauty "pollinated at full moon and high tide by Amado Vasquez,"[7] cordoned off from the wildness of the landscape outside.

When the Woolsey Fire came to Malibu, it ripped through my old neighborhood en route to the ocean. My house was one of three that didn't burn right down to the chimney column. We had sold it three months prior, and I experienced a queasy mix of relief and survivor's guilt. Didion, too, had unloaded her Trancas Canyon house just a few months before the 1978 fires and her description of the tableau might as well have been written in November, 2018, as "refugees huddled on Zuma Beach…horses caught fire…birds exploded in the air."[8] The hardiest residents just wait it out, but it was no longer our tragedy.

ENDNOTES:

1. Joan Didion, "Quiet Days in Malibu," in *The White Album* (New York: Simon & Schuster, 1979), 209.
2. Didion, "Quiet Days in Malibu," 222.
3. Joan Didion, "The Seacoast of Despair," *Slouching Towards Bethlehem* (New York: Farrar, Straus and Giroux, 1968), 213.
4. Joan Didion, "Letter from Paradise, 21' 19' N., 157' 52' W," *Slouching Towards Bethlehem* (New York: Farrar, Straus and Giroux, 1968), 187.
5. Didion, "Quiet Days in Malibu," 222.
6. Didion, "Quiet Days in Malibu," 222.
7. Didion, "Quiet Days in Malibu," 219.
8. Didion, "Quiet Days in Malibu," 223.

Tania of the Golden West

By Scott Benzel

"One journalist is worth twenty agents."[1]
—"High-level CIA official" quoted by Carl Bernstein in *Rolling Stone*

"There are rats in the avocado trees."[2]
—Joan Didion

PUBLISHED IN 1982 IN the *New York Review of Books*, Joan Didion's "Girl of the Golden West" was characteristic of her already-famous cultural pulse-taking. Guised as a review of Patricia Hearst's ghostwritten and whitewashed memoir *Every Secret Thing*, the essay also provided insight into the kidnapping, radicalization, subsequent jury trial, and the multivalent cultural fallout surrounding the case of the heiress turned radical. Didion's examination, in line with her earlier examinations of the Haight, the Diggers, the Manson family, and other radical subcultures, displayed her usual skepticism as well as, perhaps, a reluctant identification with a fellow golden girl. She wrote:

> "It was a special kind of sentimental education, a public coming-of-age…We had Patricia Campbell Hearst in

her first-communion dress, smiling, and we had Patricia Campbell Hearst in the Hibernia Bank surveillance stills, not smiling. We again had her smiling in the engagement picture, an unremarkably pretty girl in a simple dress on a sunny lawn, and we again had her not smiling in the Tania snapshot, the famous Polaroid with the M1."[3]

Didion's thoughts on Hearst would have never entered into the realpolitik of someone like Mae Brussell. Beginning in the late 1960s, Brussell hosted *Dialogue: Conspiracy*, a weekly radio show on Carmel station KLRB. Conflicting with her status as heiress to the I. Magnin department store fortune was a predominantly grassroots, working-to-middle-class allegiance and a commitment to what might be called a *Gnostic politic*, wherein hidden, subterranean forces accounted for much of the surface disorder of the time. *The Realist* magazine of February 1974 was titled "Mae Brussell's Conspiracy Newsletter" and subtitled "Why Was Patricia Hearst Kidnapped?" Where Didion saw in Hearst the accidental creation of an ideological gryphon—half-heiress, half-radical—Brussell saw sub-rosa networks of intelligence and counterintelligence forces at play. She saw the war coming home as operatives working in the CIA's Phoenix Program in Vietnam arrived back in California, clocking in on the illegal counterterrorism operation MHCHAOS, whose primary objective was to infiltrate antiwar groups and compromise students and faculty on college campuses, while others infiltrated the prisons—birthplace of Patty's kidnappers, the Symbionese Liberation Army. As agents of MHCHAOS and the FBI's COINTELPRO worked worm-in-the-apple across the country to surveil, radicalize, and otherwise disrupt the remains of the underground, the New Left, the Civil Rights, and Black Power movements, California—home of the Diggers, the Panthers, the Prison Liberation movement, innumerable cults and New

Religious movements, and the then-new SLA—was particularly ripe for their attentions.

◆◆◆

JOAN DIDION, MAE BRUSSELL, and Patricia Hearst: women of three very different generations, all of a certain class, all native to California, all attendees of the University of California at Berkeley, all members of what would come to be called the "American ruling class," all radicalized by their times. Brussell, daughter of a Los Angeles rabbi and mother of five, was radicalized by the assassination of JFK. Her long-running radio show and contributions to radical journals persistently and publicly contested the findings of the Warren Report and, later, the official stories of the assassinations of Martin Luther King Jr., Robert F. Kennedy, and the Tate-LaBianca murders. Didion, from an old California family and married to John Gregory Dunne, heir to an East Coast banking fortune, radicalized by her own neurasthenic breakdown and the increasingly sour spirit of the times. Hearst, the heiress radicalized following her kidnapping. All wrote about Hearst's abduction at the hands of the Symbionese Liberation Army and her transformation (however brief) into Tania.

◆◆◆

ON THE EVENING OF February 4, 1974, as UC Berkeley art history major Patricia Hearst and her fiancé Steven Weed ate dinner and watched *The Magician* on NBC, three heavily armed members of the Symbionese Liberation Army approached their duplex apartment on a pretty, tree-lined street. The serene, middle-class domestic scene belied Patty's lineage and her massive family wealth as well as the chaos about to be unleashed—her grandfather was heir to a mining fortune and founder of the Hearst publishing empire, her father its current chairman of the board, her family homes Wyntoon and San Simeon were legendary California piles surrounded by thousands of acres of land. Within minutes of the SLA forcibly invading the apartment, a wounded Steven Weed was scrambling through neighbors' backyards and Patty was locked in the trunk of a car stolen for the occasion.

The first tapes that the SLA released featured Patty in a dazed, stricken California drawl, beginning "Mom, Dad..." before imploring them to heed the group's demands. Within weeks, Patty joined the group, assuming the *nom de guerre* of Che Guevara's lieutenant, Tania, and the polaroid of her in shooting stance, in a black beret with an M1 leveled, was plastered across telephone poles and dorm rooms from the Bay Area to Boston. In later communiques "Mom, Dad..." became "Pig Hearsts," and Tania became the object of a previously unknown level of speculation and fantasy, forebear to "slow speed chases" and starlets' head-shaven SUV assaults.

Over the course of the next year, Tania participated in heists and bombings—eventually captured on security camera holding the M1 during a Bay Area bank robbery. Finally, alone behind the wheel of a getaway van, she emptied the clip of a submachine gun on Mel's Sporting Goods in South Los Angeles as fellow SLA members fled the store. Captured, tried, and incarcerated, Hearst was freed early and eventually pardoned, her rehabilitation complete in the way that only an heiress's rehabilitation could be, and Tania was relegated to an alternate timeline, dismissed as an aberration, product of Stockholm Syndrome or some other such disorder of modernity.

◆◆◆

CALIFORNIA IN THE 1960S and 1970s was the epicenter of a minor Gnostic revival, its high priests lowbrow sci-fi writers and the gurus of the Human Potential Movement, whose hot, often paranoiac literary style contrasted with the reserve of the Eastern Establishment. Joan Didion was unique: a hybrid East Coast skeptic and West Coast Gnostic—cool, but insistent on the reality of affect, on the fever gripping the culture, insisting, "all I knew was what I saw: flash pictures in variable sequence, images with no 'meaning.'"[4] Brussell, considered by her critics an irresponsible fantasist, was Gnostic through and through, one of the few who saw with clarity the underlying root network of intelligence operations whose existence only began to surface after Watergate and continued to spill its secrets well into the 2000s. Patty/Tania was, and remains, a cipher.

Didion's and Brussell's views on the motives behind Hearst's kidnapping are divergent to the extreme, parallax, but ultimately convergent upon a similar conclusion: Patty's kidnapping and temporary transformation operated first and foremost as symbol.

> "The image of Patricia Campbell Hearst on the FBI 'wanted' flyers was…cropped from the image of the unremarkably pretty girl in the simple dress on the sunny lawn, schematic evidence that even a golden girl could be pinned in the beam of history."[5]

Didion goes on to invoke the "unsoundable depth of the narrative,"[6] a story essentially unknowable except in the way that it operated through television and the newspapers, and, as with all of her work, the ways in which it affected her. Every fact was modified by minute physical and psychological detail, by intimate personal or family history, by grand myths and narratives. Didion's take on Hearst is filtered through California's vast mythography; the Hearst story becomes one of survival, of the Donner party, and Didion's ancestors' move out West. Patty and Tania, twin girls of the Golden West, were ultimately reflections of Didion's own inner reality. The story's symbol is the image of a burning palm tree above the South Los Angeles home in which many of the SLA burned alive during a police raid. The incident was televised and Patty watched from a room in the Disneyland hotel.

Brussell perceived in Tania another variety of symbol, the sign of a deeper external reality, a reality secretly shaping and permeating American life in the 1970s—namely, a state intelligence apparatus turned against an increasingly rebellious citizenry. On the October 13, 1971, broadcast of what was then called *Dialogue: Assassination* on KLRB, Brussell laid out her grand theory:

> "We are working with a system of what we call power: exchange of power, economic power, power over people; controlling their lives. In order to do that you disguise certain persons and send them into roles to influence; they become actors on a stage and they influence our minds in a way that is not real but effect a reality that will touch us later."[7]

Brussell's interpretation of the Tania narrative begins not with Manifest Destiny but in Vacaville prison, where SLA leader Donald DeFreeze, a former police informant, meets a CIA man fresh from Vietnam. According to Brussell (and now proven), Vacaville's Medical Facility was a major hub for both psychological experimentation and CIA infiltration of the radicalized underclass (Didion's father, a habitué of psychiatric hospitals, was treated by the doctor who later headed the facility). To Brussell, Donald Defreeze—like Lee Harvey Oswald and James Earl Ray before him—wore what is called in intelligence circles a Bad Jacket: he was not who or what he appeared to be.

At the beginning of her *Conspiracy Newsletter*, Brussell sets forth her list of "Motives for the Creation of the SLA":

"Create a national fear of terrorist organizations, and of future kidnappings, accompanied by increased bombings. Discredit communes. Discredit the poor, and test food distribution programs. Isolate prisoners from genuine reform organizations. Escalate domestic race war between blacks and whites. Discredit radical and/or leftist organizations…Turn the population into informers, who turn each other in. Discredit the FBI."[8]

If Didion's method was a trefoil of expertly constructed prose, a dead accurate parsing of the spirit of the times, Brussell's was a broadsword dialectic blowing across the police line of the real, with a sheer audacity and willingness to speculate beyond accepted fact, grounded by an uncanny ability to recognize deep patterns in the bloody chaos. She saw beneath the limited hangouts and cover stories thrown up by spooks and mass fantasists to something like the Real. This was perhaps the strongest sign of the heiress in her: she was sure of her facts, even when they were proven inaccurate. Crucially, the broad strokes of her thesis were eventually borne out in the revelations obtained through Freedom of Information Act requests and declassification. She concludes that "all of these persons involved—the major people—are agent provocateurs…We can't discuss Patty's brainwashing without looking at our own."[9]

◆◆◆

DIDION'S AND BRUSSELL'S APPROACHES are, like Patty and Tania, inverted twins. Brussell's approach suggests that the visible is always informed and orchestrated by the unseen, and that one can, through the power of intuition and imagination, perceive a hidden, material source of appearances. Like so many in the conspiracy game, Brussell appears to give too much credit to "Power's" ability to control, manipulate, and regulate known and unknown forces alike. Yet—*voilà*—these are exactly the forces that bubble forth years later in declassified documents.

Didion, on the other hand, is entranced by the outer chaos but sees its roots lying always within the self, bubbling up from the subterranean ocean of myth, history, persona. These outer events/myths are almost always myths of disorder, of the breakdown of the narrative, and seem to reflect the inner turmoil following her nervous breakdown, the events leading up to it, the decades of fallout...

Like Mailer, Thompson, and the other New Journalists, Didion aspired to a new form of journalistic truth, one that openly admitted and readily engaged the filters of subjectivity, of personal history, obsessions, and addictions. Brussell aspired instead to a sort of depth journalism, to reach beneath the surface of events to the invisible seismic forces causing them.

The problem with both forms of journalism is the problem of the Real itself—specifically, human perception's limited ability to access it. And journalism, like ourselves, is always lost in the past, always trailing the forces of history as they erode the present itself, and in the impossible paradoxes of lived experience.

ENDNOTES:

1. Carl Bernstein, "The CIA and the Media," *Rolling Stone*, October 20, 1977, http: carlbernstein.com/magazine_cia_and_media

2. Paraphrased quote from Michiko Kakutani, "Joan Didion: Staking Out California," *The New York Times,* June 10, 1979. https://www.nytimes.com/1979/06/10/books/didion-calif.html

3. Joan Didion, "Girl of the Golden West," in *After Henry* (New York: Simon & Schuster, 1992), 96.

4. Joan Didion, "The White Album," in *The White Album* (New York: Simon & Schuster, 1979), 13.

5. Didion, "Girl of the Golden West," 97.

6. Didion, "Girl of the Golden West," 97.

7. Mae Brussell, "Why was Patty Hearst Kidnapped?," *The Realist*, February 1974.

8. Brussell, "Why was Patty Hearst Kidnapped?."

9. Brussell, "Why was Patty Hearst Kidnapped?"

West of the West Wing of Oz:
A Sentimental Journey

By Ezrha Jean Black

"The ceremony of innocence is drowned..."[1]
—W. B. Yeats, "The Second Coming"

"Pay no attention to that man behind the curtain...I am Oz, the great and powerful."[2]
—Ryerson, Langley, et al., after L. Frank Baum, *The Wizard of Oz*

FOR THOSE OF US of a certain generation, the transition to Los Angeles had the kind of aura or magical logic most frequently encountered in a dream. We slept—on a plane, in the back of a car, or perhaps in a train sleeper—and the next thing we knew, we were in a very different place. Alien and alienating, yet just managing to conform to the dream logic of the preceding five days, or hours. Sphinxes and savages, rough beasts and messiahs had been there ahead of us, scattering a vast machinery in their wake, through which, between far-flung landmarks natural and man-made, we picked out places that might shelter us from the unrelenting sun. As far as my siblings and I could tell, these were mostly movie theatres, coffee shops, steakhouses, cocktail lounges, and Ralph's Supermarket.

We had no idea where we were exactly. We knew that some piece of actual magic had drawn our parents there; that they had something to do with creating the dream visions projected upon those cinema screens, or at least the instruments and processes that allowed others to create them. We took none of this for granted. Still, motoring down long concourses flanked on either side by the large blank or billboarded walls behind which so much of this magic was being made, swept finally through canyons or into suburban cul-de-sacs, we realized that we were being initiated into an opaque social exchange, surrendering our trust to a system, an industry, we could never entirely grasp.

It was the late 1960s in what was then still referred to as the world's "film capital." We were soon made aware of other industries that filled out this landscape, including one or two that would have a similar cultural impact. But few encompassed the essential terms and conditions of this social contract quite so comprehensively—governed by a far more prosaic dream logic, in which everything was negotiable, from personal identity to the dream itself. In this place where natural and human history seemed to have been finessed or sidestepped, reality itself might be seen as negotiable.

The ceremonies of this commerce, both public and private, took many forms, from informal negotiation to legal arbitration or adjudication; seduction and celebration; also deception and corruption; and occasionally intimidation. The road between deal memo and final cut might be long and labyrinthine; and the paving stones costly, whether lead or gold. For many years they seemed mostly about establishing or legitimizing a kind of control, and reinforcing a certain hierarchy.

It was probably around this time of transition, between the ceremonies of innocence and disillusionment, that my brother and I became aware of Joan Didion—first by way of the odd magazine piece, and soon thereafter with the publication of *Play It As It Lays*, which found its way into my brother's hands and was quickly passed on to me. It was a voice and perception of reality we connected with immediately (even though we had only just learned how to drive). We devoured her *Esquire* columns, and later, pretty much everything she wrote. There were cultural politics implicit in some of that journalism and even the novels, and it was not surprising that Didion should make the transition between writing about sociopolitical attitudes and their particular tone-deaf manifestations in Hollywood and elsewhere, to observing the American political process and some of its driving personalities and ideologues firsthand.

Much of this writing is anthologized in *Political Fictions*, and taking the measure of everything that has happened between the decades before the millennium and now, its continuity and resonance with the totality of her work, and its resonance with the current political and cultural moment—between Didion's first apprehensions of the "blood-dimmed tide," to borrow her own quotation, and the "fables about American experience"[3] underpinning its political process—are doubly striking. "We tell ourselves stories to live," she reminded us early in *The White Album*. "Or at least we do for a while…"[4]

Parallel to these stories, our performance of ceremony is a way of asserting control over a narrative that has no certain endpoint. Just how uncertain, Didion was to discover in brutal fashion not long after *Political Fictions* was published. Her essay on the collective narrative pieced out of the criminal prosecution and—most importantly—the media coverage and its underlying context of historic and urban legend that became the story of the Central Park Five, could not ultimately reach the truth, nor the brutal reality of systemic persecution, brutality, and injustice imposed upon African Americans in the United States.

Ceremonies touch on profound beliefs and cherished ideals, our highest aspirations—the commencement address, the Nobel Prize ceremonies. They also allude to our greatest fears, our reckoning with fate—"to have and to hold, in sickness or in health, 'til death do you part." Or the essential preliminary to official judgment—"Do you swear to tell the truth…?" They can function as a screen, filtering or hiding such fears from view, or serving as that upon which we project our most intimidating fabulations. In this respect, a ceremony is not unlike an iconostasis upon which our gods and heroes are represented, but which closes us off from the priestly transactions with the divine. Didion references religious ceremony specifically in a passage from that same Central Park Five essay ("New York: Sentimental Journeys") about a witness in one of the trials and the sacrificial image of the crime victim, Trisha Meili ("The Central Park Jogger"), built up by contemporary news accounts. The intersection of religion and politics is no accident. American political life is replete with ceremony—from voting booth to the executive inaugural.

The disasters that have ushered in this century have come largely without ceremony—unless you count George W. Bush's infamous "Mission Accomplished" reception of the aircraft carrier, *Abraham Lincoln*, returning from the Persian Gulf after its participation in initiating a war—whose "mission" was neither "accomplished" nor even convincingly articulated. The screens went noticeably dark as that mission dragged on, with cameras barred from such military ceremonies as the reception of returning coffins at Dover Air Force Base. In fact, the black screen or wall might be considered the hallmark of the George W. Bush presidential administration, with its reliance on black sites, black ops, black projects, and "ghost detainees"—that last term signaling an intention to erase identity, to purge history.

For a time, I wondered whether, in the wake of the 2001 suicide attacks on the World Trade Center and the collapse of its twin towers, we would see (and hear) a fresh appreciation, valuation, even devotion to the spoken and written word; it seemed possible for a brief moment. But the culture of distraction, ever so powerful in the West, drowned that hope in emojis, Twitter bots, and assorted mass digital hacks. Long after the fact, I now wonder whether distraction had itself replaced words—descriptive, prescriptive, ceremonial, or contractual—as the means of control. It is not unremarkable that it was the Bush White House and State Department's insistence on ignoring the factual "story" that led directly to the news story—their failure to consider critical intelligence indicating the prospect of a catastrophic terror strike on key financial and government power centers in the United States. But even before the "purge" of history, this was part of a longer prehistory of American economic and geopolitical interests in the Middle East and their long-term ramifications.

In the intervening years, we've become more adept at the ceremonies of mourning, farewell, forgiveness—the marches and candlelight vigils; the memorials. But these are by definition unequal exchanges, a pledge of faith for which we're promised nothing in return beyond a vague solace. We might just as well be in L. Frank Baum's or MGM's Oz, where, having reneged on his offer to transport Dorothy home in exchange for the Wicked Witch's broom, the carnival barker passing himself off as the great and powerful Oz essentially tries to console her by offering her a lifetime of green-tinted lenses. Nothing changes except the way we might see things. In the hands of demagogues, these are effectively ceremonies of control, even subjugation. Black screens are bright again and bleeding electric color. But nothing passes for solace and there is no forgiveness.

It was not mere coincidence that the Oz presented in the 1978 film version of *The Wiz* was an eccentric stylization of New York City itself—including the World Trade Center as Emerald City (in relative infancy as buildings go and—like Michael Jackson's "Scarecrow"—not to survive long past adulthood). It is, as Didion herself notes, at "the heart of the way the city presents itself... eight million stories and all the same story, each devised to obscure not only the city's actual tensions of race and class but also, more significantly, the civic and commercial arrangements that rendered those tensions irreconcilable."[5]

But in 1989 there was one carnival barker in New York already keen on exploiting those "irreconcilable tensions" and spoiling for a fight to capitalize on them. The Central Park Five case didn't exactly introduce Donald Trump to New York—he was already notorious as an unscrupulous real estate developer—but it broke his brand of hate speech coupled with a peculiar penchant for self-aggrandizement wide open. "BRING BACK THE DEATH PENALTY. BRING BACK OUR POLICE!" screamed the headline of a full-page ad that he ran in all four of the city's major newspapers.

The police, of course, hadn't gone anywhere. They were running the case—almost stampeding it as it turned out, under the whip-cracking desperation of the Manhattan Assistant District Attorney's office. Between a city's hysteria and prosecutorial over-zealotry, the five were convicted in 1990. By 2002, having essentially served full sentences, the five would see their convictions vacated in the State Supreme Court. The City would admit no wrongdoing in later financial settlements with the exonerated individuals. And neither would Donald Trump.

No one in 1989 could have anticipated that a figure usually relegated to the society pages, and frequently ridiculed in them, might in the next century—after Reagan, Clinton, two Bushes, and finally Obama—assume that office. But then no one in 1989 would have imagined that within another fifteen years, Donald Trump would become a star of so-called "reality" television.

We always knew the world outside Oz was not so forgiving. We're an emerald-and-sapphire speck in a cosmos where stars implode and explode in the blink of an eye. States may deploy personnel and armaments to destroy each other; multinational corporations may dispatch vessels and machinery to plunder the planet's resources, to alter or destroy sections of it entirely; species may fall by the millions and humans with them; and the universe will go right on as if none of it had happened in the first place. The denizens of Oz understand this and go right on, not in defiance of thermodynamics but in defiance of human society. To the extent they remain within that society as its governors, executives, lawmakers, and administrators, this defiance represents a betrayal of trust, a fundamental breach of faith.

In the same way our grand wizards seem determined to ignore, if not defy, the physical limits of the planet and curve of the universe, the speed of technological change and technology itself have both compressed the cultural geography into a kind of global megalopolis, if not the global village McLuhan once envisioned, and flattened history's "story arc." This has complicated both the task of narrating the stories that become our history and the way we receive those stories. Didion makes this the fulcrum of the reporting and essays that comprise "The West Wing of Oz"—the way in which a story—in this particular instance, a massacre of civilians in the Salvadoran village, El Mozote—might be "exposed to the light and then allowed to fall back into the dark."[6] Her larger subject was the way in which American interventions in disparate foreign conflicts have functioned as screens upon which American presidents projected an alternative narrative of leadership.

The parallels between the post-Reagan and post-Patriot Act Bushes—from their respective choices in stagecraft to their willful inattention to imminent threats—are grimly ironic. I will own up to the no less ironic fact that during those black screen years, I, along with a critical mass of demographically significant viewers, escaped to my own "over-the-rainbow" place in Aaron Sorkin's NBC series, *The West Wing*, with Martin Sheen playing a president the polar opposite of Ronald Reagan or George W. Bush. The parallels highlighted by Didion's observations on the Reagan White House, on the other hand, are with that place behind the soundstage wall. Didion discusses the ceremonial aspects of Reagan's executive style, as well as his staff's treatment of the Oval Office routine, as an ongoing production shoot. We can see that Reagan used the secure routine of daily briefings, meetings, and photo opportunities to reinforce an illusion of control. But more crucially, she focuses on Reagan's idea of the reciprocity of civic good faith that defined how he saw his relationship with the American public—or more precisely, the idealized character he thought he embodied as president.

It's the old problem, as Didion saw it, of "licking the script."[7] How do we move that central idealized character from the second to the third act? (And, parenthetically, how do we get an audience or constituency to care?) Didion saw well beyond that problem to the problem of the "story" itself and the underlying narrative it promoted. Between 1991 and 2000, when she wrote "God's

Country" (touching on the pernicious influence of evangelical Christianity on American politics), she more or less put her finger right on it: the patriarchal revanche—and all the iconography, smoke, incense, and incendiary devices surrounding it.

"God's Country" is resurgent in 2019, even if half of it seems to be under water at any given moment. (Leave it to the next "carnival barker" to build an ark—or balloon—to sail its hapless citizens out.) But there is no real story to this green-screen mythology—no story arc for the ark of fools; and nothing remotely approaching an idealized character. Instead we have something like a *Pokémon* blown up life-size—the Trump baby balloon will do. The actual West Wing in 2019 seems more reality show than the ersatz "boardroom" that served as the set for the NBC reality show, *The Apprentice*—the vehicle that made Trump a star. Ceremony didn't "drown" so much as burn up with the carnage of Trump's inaugural address. All we have left to stand in for presidential ceremony in 2019 are the endlessly repeated catchphrases, recycled rhetorical tropes, retweets, dog whistles, and naked lies. To which the rest of us can only chant mournfully: *Mea culpa, mea culpa, mea maxima culpa.*

Some of us still try to "lick the script" in 2019, moving between our own second and third acts and trying not to break faith—with ourselves, with our country, with Los Angeles— itself moving into its fourth act, which sometimes seems like a dusty mirage. In the decades that have followed "The West Wing of Oz," we find ourselves crossing a decaying suspension bridge, performing a ceremony of hope against our withered innocence, trying not to drown or combust in that last mirage. *Fade to black.*

ENDNOTES:

1. William Butler Yeats, "The Second Coming," in *The Collected Poems of W. B. Yeats* (New York: The MacMillan Company, 1956.

2. *The Wizard of Oz,* film, directed by Victor Fleming (1939; Los Angeles: Metro-Goldwyn-Mayer).

3. Joan Didion, "A Foreword," in *Political Fictions* (New York; Alfred A. Knopf, 2001), 7

4. Joan Didion, "The White Album," in *The White Album* (New York: Simon & Schuster, 1979), 11.

5. Joan Didion, "New York: Sentimental Journeys," in *After Henry* (New York: Simon & Schuster, 1992), 279–80.

6. Joan Didion, "The West Wing of Oz," in *Political Fictions*, (New York; Alfred A. Knopf, 2001), 69.

7. Didion, "The West Wing of Oz," 111.

Contributors

Alysia Abbott is the author of *Fairyland: A Memoir of My Father* (W.W. Norton, 2013). Her work has appeared in *The New York Times, The Boston Globe, LitHub, OUT, Vogue,* and elsewhere. She lives in Cambridge, MA with her family.

Scott Benzel is an artist and writer living in Los Angeles. He is the author of ISBN 978-0-9913772-0-6, 2016; *Sonatine Bureaucratique*, 2018; and *Performance Scores*, 2019, all published by Los Angeles Contemporary Archive Press.

Ezrha Jean Black is a writer living and working in Los Angeles. Her favorite book in childhood was *The Wonderful Wizard of Oz*; it still is.

Steph Cha is the author of four novels, the Juniper Song mysteries and *Your House Will Pay* (Ecco). She's the noir editor for *LA Review of Books* and a regular contributor to the *Los Angeles Times* and *USA Today*.

Michelle Chihara teaches contemporary American literature and creative writing at Whittier College. Her fiction and prose have appeared in a variety of publications, from *Mother Jones* to

Postmodern Culture. She edits the Economics & Finance section of *LA Review of Books*.

Dan Crane is a writer, professional air guitarist (retired), and author of *To Air is Human: One Man's Quest to Become the World's Greatest Air Guitarist* (Riverhead Books).

Joe Donnelly is an award-winning journalist, editor and short-story writer and the author of the collection *L.A. Man: Profiles from a Big City and a Small World* (Rare Bird).

Jori Finkel covers contemporary art for *The New York Times* and *The Art Newspaper* from Los Angeles. Her new book *It Speaks to Me* (Prestel) features fifty artists on artworks that inspire them from museums around the world.

Heather John Fogarty is a Los Angeles-based writer whose work has appeared in *Australian Vogue, Bon Appétit, LA Review of Books*, and *Los Angeles Magazine*, and has been featured on NPR. She teaches Media, Food, and Culture at USC Annenberg and is a former James Beard Restaurant Awards Judge.

Ann Friedman is a journalist who covers gender, politics, technology, and culture. She hosts the podcasts *Call Your Girlfriend* and *Going Through It*.

Monica Corcoran Harel writes for *The New York Times, Marie Claire*, and *The Hollywood Reporter*. She has authored best sellers, like *Love Yourself. Love Your Life* with the cast of *Queer Eye*—and launched Prettyripe.com for women over forty who kick ass.

Jessica Hundley is an LA-based writer, director, and producer. She has authored books for Taschen, Chronicle, and others. In her journalism and directing work, she explores art, music, and film with a focus on counterculture, metaphysics, and psychedelia.

Linda Immediato, a born and bred New Yorker, discovered Joan Didion's work while attending journalism school. It inspired both her career, which includes writing and editing for *Gourmet*, *LA Weekly*, and *Angeleno*, and a move to Los Angeles. She is currently the style editor of *Los Angeles* magazine.

Christine Lennon is a freelance magazine writer and editor living in Los Angeles. Her first novel, *The Drifter* (William Morrow), was published in 2017.

Tracy McMillan is a television writer, memoirist, relationship expert, and host of the reality show *Family or Fiance* on OWN-TV. Her viral TEDx talk, "The Person You Really Need to Marry," has more than eleven million views.

Steffie Nelson has written about style and culture for publications including *The New York Times*, *LA Review of Books*, the *Los Angeles Times*, and many others. She recently coauthored *Judson: Innovation in Stained Glass* with David Judson (Angel City Press).

Caroline Ryder is a British screenwriter, ghostwriter, and journalist based in Echo Park, Los Angeles.

Lauren Sandler is a journalist, essayist, and best-selling author based in New York. Her third book, *This Is All I Got* (Random House), has been shortlisted for the Lukas Prize.

Joshua Wolf Shenk's work has appeared in *Riverteeth*, *The Atlantic*, *Harper's*, and *The New Yorker*. He is the author of *Lincoln's Melancholy* (Mariner Books) and *Powers of Two* (Mariner Books). He is editor-in-chief of *The Believer* and artistic and executive director of the Beverly Rogers, Carol C. Harter Black Mountain Institute at UNLV.

Stacie Stukin is a journalist and essayist who was born and raised in Los Angeles. Her byline has appeared in the *Los Angeles Times*, *The New York Times*, *W Magazine*, and *Architectural Digest*. She is currently working on a novel.

Sarah Tomlinson is the author of the father-daughter memoir, *Good Girl* (Gallery Books). She has ghostwritten or cowritten seventeen books, including the *NYT* best seller *Fast Girl* (Dey Street Books) with Suzy Favor Hamilton. Her essays have appeared in *Marie Claire*, *MORE*, *Publisher's Weekly*, Salon.com, and others.

Catherine Wagley writes about art and culture in Los Angeles. Her work has recently appeared in the *Los Angeles Times*, *ART News*, and *Artforum* and she is a contributing editor at *Momus* and *Contemporary Art Review Los Angeles* (*CARLA*).

Margaret Wappler has written for *Elle*, *Washington Post*, *Slate*, *The New York Times* and many other publications. Her debut novel, *Neon Green*, was shortlisted for the VCU Cabell First Novelist Award, and was praised as "witty and entertaining" by the *Los Angeles Times*.

Marc Weingarten is the author of *Thirsty: William Mulholland, California Water, and The Real Chinatown* (Rare Bird); *The Gang that Wouldn't Write Straight* (Crown); and *Station to Station* (Gallery Books). He lives in Benedict Canyon.

Su Wu is a writer and curator living in Mexico City with her partner and their daughter. She is an art editor for *n+1*.

Selected Bibliography

Books by Joan Didion

NOVELS

Run River. New York: Ivan Obolensky, 1963.
Play It As It Lays. New York: Farrar, Straus and Giroux, 1970.
A Book of Common Prayer. New York: Simon & Schuster, 1977.
Democracy. New York: Simon & Schuster, 1984.
The Last Thing He Wanted. New York: Alfred A. Knopf, 1996.

ESSAYS

Slouching Towards Bethlehem. New York: Farrar, Straus and Giroux, 1968.
The White Album. New York: Simon & Schuster, 1979.
After Henry. New York: Simon & Schuster, 1992.
Political Fictions. New York: Alfred A. Knopf, 2001.
Fixed Ideas: America Since 9.11. New York: New York Review of Books, 2003.

NONFICTION

Salvador. New York: Simon & Schuster, 1983.
Miami. New York: Simon & Schuster, 1987.
Where I Was From. New York: Alfred A. Knopf, 2003.
The Year of Magical Thinking. New York: Alfred A. Knopf, 2005.
Blue Nights. New York: Alfred A. Knopf, 2011.
South and West: From a Notebook. New York: Alfred A. Knopf, 2017.

Selected References

BOOKS

Daugherty, Tracy. *The Last Love Song: A Biography of Joan Didion.* New York: St. Martin's Press, 2015.

Nelson, Deborah, *Tough Enough: Arbus, Arendt, Didion, McCarthy, Sontag, Weil.* Chicago: University of Chicago Press, 2017.

Parker, Scott F., editor. *Conversations with Joan Didion.* Jackson: University Press of Mississippi, 2018.

Weingarten, Marc. *The Gang That Wouldn't Write Straight: Wolfe, Thompson, Didion and the New Journalism Revolution.* New York: Crown, 2006.

FILM

Dunne, Griffin, director. *Joan Didion: The Center Will Not Hold* (documentary film). Netflix, 2017.

Acknowledgments

FIRSTLY, THANK YOU TO Joan Didion, a most generous muse. Thank you to all the writers, who delivered like the pros they are, and made this an exciting and enlightening journey. Special thanks to Michelle Chihara, Joe Donnelly, Heather John Fogarty, Monica Corcoran Harel, Jessica Hundley, Caroline Ryder, Stacie Stukin, Sarah Tomlinson, and Marc Weingarten, who offered support above and beyond their fine work. *Slouching Towards Los Angeles* would not exist without Zoe Crosher, whose art always inspires new ways of looking at California, and the organization LAND—especially Laura Hyatt—who provided a forum where the concept could take form. I am grateful to Eric Rayman, who kindly shared his legal expertise; Jodi Wille, who offered pearls of publishing wisdom; gracious connector Laurel Stearns; and Kimberly Brooks, J. C. Gabel, Alexandra Grant, and Thao Nguyen, for their early enthusiasm for this project. Finally, many thanks to Tyson Cornell and Rare Bird, who said "let's do it!" and meant it.